THE TRUTH
—IS NOT—
WHAT WE
WERE TAUGHT

A Personal Journey of Breaking Free
from the Spiritual Lies We've Inherited

LENORA HOAG

Ordering Information:
Quantity sales. Special discounts are available on quantity purchases by corporations, associations, and others. Orders by U.S. trade bookstores and wholesalers. For details, contact the publisher through the website above.

Editing by The Pro Book Editor
Interior and Cover Design by IAPS.rocks

ISBN: 978-1-7365929-1-5

     1. Main category—RELIGION / Faith
     2. Other category—RELIGION / Christian Living / Personal Growth
     3. Other category—RELIGION / Christian Theology / Ecclesiology

First Edition

TABLE OF CONTENTS

DEDICATION

First, to my Heavenly Father, I give thanks and praise because without Him I can do nothing. He is my everything. And next, I dedicate this book to my dear husband of over forty years and my sweet mother, both of whom have been my companions and constant encouragers, especially in this most recent journey of discovering our Heavenly Father's will.

I also dedicate this book to my children and especially to my dear grandchildren for whom I pray daily that their hearts are circumcised (a heart in which the outer covering is symbolically cut away so that one can feel) to love their Creator with all their being.

And finally, I dedicate this book to those who have begun their journey, like us, back to their Heavenly Father's Word, to truly learn what it means to walk as our Messiah walked.

PREFACE

W HAT IF, OVER THE COURSE of a few hours, you discovered something that changed your perspective about what you had always known (or thought you had always known) your entire life?

What you are about to read is a story, my story, of a journey that began about nine years ago. I pray it will challenge you. And I know it may very well take you on a roller coaster of emotions from anger and disbelief to even a few feelings of sadness. It's similar to the stages of grieving, of letting someone or something go. But for sure, if you are able to lay hold of the prize I am challenging you to grasp and hang on to it, you will begin to experience a joy and a peace that are unspeakable, like the light of a new day at dawn as it shines ever brighter and brighter.

What if the words of the Scriptures are true, yet we have misinterpreted them for years? Can you imagine that what you have been taught and believed all your life may not be the truth? What does His Word say about deception? Do we have an enemy who will stop at nothing to twist the truth to have us serve him, thus driving a wedge of separation between ourselves and our Heavenly Father? Does Scripture speak to the fact that we could be lied to? And does Scripture verify that truth would be lost, and blurred lines between truth and lies would then be cleared up again, at some point in time?

These are the questions I will answer, and more, throughout the pages of this book while I am telling the story of the unexpected journey I found myself taking in the fall of 2011.

Our heavenly Father is continuously molding and shaping us through our experiences and through His Word when we let Him. I've had many stops and starts of allowing Him to do this as I'm sure most of you have too. And at the same time, I've always had my eye on the world arena for how our societies move closer and closer to those days described in Matthew 24 that have to take place before the coming of our Savior. So now, because of my experiences through the last few years and because of what I am seeing in our world today, I knew I needed to share what I have learned and how these experiences relate to the events just around the corner.

I've always recorded my thoughts, feelings, and discoveries since I was a child, but have never attempted to write a book except for some little handmade, rustic-looking books I made out of paper sacks one time. How I wish I still had them to see just what I had written on those tiny pages. I love writing down the musings of my heart, soul, and mind and have often prayed for the opportunity to share and inspire others with the things I have written, with the words He has given me, just as a musician touches and inspires the listener with the words and melody of his songs. It has taken years of living (almost 60!) and searching, re-searching, reflecting, and writing to come to this point. As I sat looking through the pages of my notes, preparing to begin this endeavor, my thoughts were: *This is personal. Where do I start?*

Before telling you of this journey, I first need to share what prompted me to start writing this book. It started when I was inspired to write a letter of admonishment to our local pastors.

I asked my dear husband, Kevin, for advice, counsel, and help. Together, we discussed, corrected, and reviewed what I had written. It took four months to finally finish that letter. Much research, prayer, and thought went into what I still feel was a brave step that our flesh definitely did not want to complete. Who did we think we were to admonish men and women of renown who are led to be the spiritual leaders and teachers of our community? It was a bold move, I know, but the prompting of our Heavenly Father often works that way. I'm sure many of you can relate. He gets us out of our comfort zone. This was the confidence that I needed and that He used to prompt me to write in book form many of the same thoughts, scriptures, and encouragements that we shared with our community pastors. And these same truths relate to the telling of our journey in the following pages.

I pray you will test everything written in this book by humbly opening your copy of His Word more than you have ever done in your life! Keep it close and follow along....

CHAPTER 1
What if you found out Christmas is pagan?

EFORE I JUMP RIGHT IN and answer this question, I
need to give you some background about me and my
family that I'm sure many of you can relate to.

We had always identified as Christians. My husband Kevin,
my mother, and I were raised in Christian homes with the understanding that it was good and right to believe in our Heavenly Father and His Son and to attend church. We celebrated
the holidays much like everybody else and never thought about
Christmas being wrong, except in the sense that commercialism
seemed to have taken over.

At bedtime while I was growing up, my mother had taught
me Psalm 23, the names of all the books of the Bible in order,
and the Ten Commandments. And like many little girls, I had
idolized my daddy. I carried an uncanny fear of losing him when
I was young. I knew, even in my childlike spirit, that this was
wrong—to put another person before my Heavenly Father. I
remember thinking in my heart, *I'm sorry, Father, but I love my
daddy more.* And I did! It was true. Then, at age seventeen, I
met my soon-to-be husband. I had grown up, so I thought, and
transferred the center of my world to Kevin. We were married as
soon as I graduated from high school. I started college while we
both worked. We were so young. Kevin was twenty-one, and I

was eighteen. We hadn't settled into married life very well at all when we found out we were expecting. Kevin was excited. I was not. And both of our families were excited, so I fell into what I'd thought was acceptance of this upcoming life change.

The day we took our perfect, beautiful daughter home, fear and anxiety hit me hard. I was afraid this beautiful child would be taken from me through SIDS because of feelings and thoughts I had suppressed during the pregnancy of not really wanting a child at that difficult and early stage of our marriage. All those fears and thoughts came flooding back, and I felt trapped and then guilty. I felt aged beyond my years and thought my whole life was over. Out of fear, I watched our little daughter sleep and breathe for four days and nights straight. The lack of sleep alone was enough to make anyone psychotic.

When I became fearful of picking up knives and scissors, I knew I needed help. My mother recognized the postpartum depression and took me to her family doctor. He said, "This is more than postpartum depression. It is postpartum psychosis. She cannot be left alone." I was put on Xanax and Elavil, we moved in with Kevin's parents, and I began counseling with a close friend and mentor of my dad's who was an understanding and wise Filipino pastor at a Methodist counseling center in Dallas. I began to sleep at night and forced myself to eat and care for my baby girl during the day. We were able to move back home after a couple of weeks. But still, the deep, dark cloud of depression and anxiety attacks that hit without warning, and with overwhelming heart-racing, out-of-control thoughts, continued. I was barely functioning and cried out daily to my Savior for help. I searched for relief in my Scriptures and hung onto several verses, repeating their words in my mind. The following verse gave me the most comfort.

> These things I have spoken to you, that in Me you may have peace. In the world you will have

tribulation; but be of good cheer, I have overcome the world. (John 16:33 NKJV)

It was a strange comfort for me to have this warning that wasn't sugarcoated, informing me that life wasn't supposed to be perfect and there would be trouble. Also, knowing that He overcame anything and everything this world could dish out was comforting. I knew my Savior was the only one who could get me out of that horrible state of existence because He was the only one who could really know and feel all my pain. I quickly realized this was something neither my dad nor Kevin could get me out of, no matter how much I had idolized them.

I wanted the pain to end. And truthfully, I wanted to die. I remember thinking I would have paid someone to shoot me. This was suffering in a way I had never known before and couldn't seem to overcome. Yet I knew my life was not mine to take. I did not give myself life and had no right to take it. So I learned how to keep on surviving one day at a time. And many times, it felt like it took everything I had to survive one more minute! Out of desperation, I learned how to fight the negative thoughts with truth—Scriptures—and to praise myself for even the smallest accomplishments of daily living, like getting out of bed, showering, and getting dressed. This mental battle was exhausting work. One negative thought would produce such fear that I felt it in the pit of my stomach. I had to train myself to push all negative thinking out of my mind and replace it with Scripture. I also found I couldn't lie down and close my eyes during the daytime, or my heart would pound and my mind would race. So no matter how tired I was, I didn't lie down until bedtime.

After six months of fighting and struggling to survive, I found the panic attacks lessening, but the depression was still just as strong. I wanted to feel better—yesterday! But no matter how much I cried out to my Savior, no matter how much I wanted to feel like myself again, to be relieved of the pain and to feel some sense of happiness and normality, it just wasn't happening. I finally reached a point of surrender and changed the way I had been praying. Instead of begging for relief, I gave up and told my Savior, *"If You can use me in this horrible state that I am in, and You want me to stay in this deep, dark hellhole, then I will stay."* Staying in that deep, dark hole was the last thing I wanted to do. Yet I sensed that maybe someday He could use me to help someone else.

Do you know what happened next? The very next morning when I woke up, over fifty percent of my deep, dark cloud had lifted! I was shocked! Is this what He had been waiting for and had been trying to teach me? I began to realize that He had been trying to be first in my life, to take center stage and for me to love Him with all my heart, soul, mind, and strength—to trust Him completely—no more idolizing my dad or my husband or putting any other person before Him. After six more months, I emerged from that horrible state of existence a stronger, more positive-thinking person than I had been my entire life!

That's what He had been waiting for—my total surrender to lay down my life for His sake, His purpose, His will, not mine! Then I understood what King David had been talking about when he said, "It was good for me to have been afflicted." I'd always known our Heavenly Father chastens those He loves (Proverbs 3:12 and Hebrews 12:5-6). Years later, I ran across the following verse

> And do not be conformed to this world, but be transformed by the renewing of your mind...
> (Romans 12:2a NKJV)

I found that I had literally, out of desperation, lived those words! My Heavenly Father had transformed me by the renewing of my mind. It had been a hard and tough road, but the reward was greater than I could have ever imagined.

As the years progressed, my faith and reliance on His Word

increased. Kevin and I continued to serve our church families, first at the Baptist church and then years later at a Pentecostal church. During this time, our own family grew with the addition of two more beautiful daughters. While they were growing, we served in several different areas, from teaching pre-K and youth Sunday school classes to taking teens on mission trips and cooking for various functions and fundraisers. Our girls served right along with us, often showing their own individual talents that the Father had blessed them with. We felt privileged and honored as our girls matured and then years later as they blessed us with four wonderful grandchildren. Our family kept us busy even though we both worked outside the home for many years. Sharing life and making memories with our children and especially our grandchildren has been such a blessing for us.

So now you may ask why I shared all of this at the beginning of a chapter about Christmas. Here's the reason.

Life could not have been better, and then suddenly it began to change. Several times over the period of about a year, I would periodically hear in my thoughts—or you might say, in my spirit—these words: *"Love Me with all your heart, soul, mind, and strength."* Immediately, I'd respond with, *"Father, you know that I love you with all my heart. I'm doing your work. I'm serving family and church. And I am satisfied with that."* At the time, I was very busy taking care of my mother and dad until he passed away of Alzheimer's. We never got to share this new journey of truth with him, but I'll share more about him in the next chapter. I continued with babysitting grandchildren and helping my daughter and son-in-law with their children's church ministry. And through all this, I would still hear those words, *"Love Me with all your heart, soul, mind, and strength."* Each time I heard them and responded in the same way, I never wondered if any of my actions needed changing. I felt no nudging or prompting to question or change anything. I kept walking the same walk.

Then one evening in the fall of that year, I was sitting at my computer and had the thought to do an internet search for the question, "Is Christmas pagan?" Pagan, or paganism, is a term that was used by early Christians to refer to an irreligious or hedonistic person or belief system, and also to describe non-Christians who worshipped false gods—idolatry. As I read the internet search results, I was shocked, especially with what I saw on websites that were historical and not affiliated with any religious or denominational group. I thought, *What reason would encyclopedias have for lying about the pagan aspects of Christmas? How could we not have known this?*

These encyclopedias showed the origin of our traditions of bringing a tree inside our homes and decorating it, hanging wreaths, gift-giving on or around the date of December 25, the yule log, lights (candles back then) used during the holidays, and even the days of merriment—all being the practices of ancient pagan religions dedicated to the worship of their gods, including the Roman god Saturn. Their celebrations took place during the winter solstice, long before our Messiah's birth.

This is a link to what I found in the *Encyclopedia Britannica* showing the Saturnalia, the most popular of Roman festivals directly influencing Christmas and New Year's celebrations, with Christmas being celebrated on the birthday of the unconquered sun. You can read more details at this website: **https://www.britannica.com/topic/Saturnalia-Roman-festival**

Below is just a brief sample of what I found on one of the encyclopedia websites:

> Thus Christians began to celebrate Christ's birthday on December 25, which was already an important pagan festival, in order to safely adapt to Roman customs while still honoring Jesus' birth.
>
> This is how Christmas came to be celebrated on the Roman holiday of Saturnalia, and it was from the

pagan holiday that many of the customs of Christmas had their roots. The celebrations of Saturnalia included the making and giving of small presents (*Saturnalia et Sigillarcia*). This holiday was observed over a series of days beginning December 17 (the birthday of Saturn) and ending on December 25 (the birthday of Sol Invictus, the "Unconquered Sun"). The combined festivals resulted in an extended winter holiday season. Business was postponed and even slaves feasted. There was drinking, gambling and singing, and nudity was relatively common. It was the "best of days" according to the poet Catullus.[1]

I also learned that Christmas was even outlawed in early American colonies by many of our founding fathers. This wasn't that long ago! What did they know that we don't know? So I encourage you to do your own internet search for the historical and pagan roots of Christmas, as there is much more evidence than I can quote in this chapter.

After researching websites both for and against this holiday tradition, I immediately thought, *He can't be happy with this!* I knew my Creator is set apart from all unrighteousness. He is pure. And I've always known that He is very jealous! I could not see Him being even a little bit okay with pagan traditions and holidays being included in our worship of Him and His Son, no matter what our reasons for doing so and no matter how these traditions evolved into what we call them today. I realized that I had been unknowingly celebrating Christmas from my own perspective and not from His. Then I heard those words again. *"Love Me with all your heart, soul, mind, and strength."* And again, my response was, *"You know I love you."* Next came

1   New World Encyclopedia contributors, "Christmas," New World Encyclopedia, **https://www.newworldencyclopedia.org/p/index.php?title= Christmas&oldid=1032977.**

something else I had never heard before. Quickly, clearly, and firmly, He said, *"Prove it!"*

I knew exactly what He was telling me to do! I had to remove everything associated with the Christmas holiday tradition from my house that night! I didn't stop to think about how much I loved this holiday, with its traditional foods, smells, sights, sounds, feelings, music, colors, shopping, and family times. All I knew was that I had to be obedient. I had to get all my Christmas decorations, from the old antique ornaments to my children's handmade ornaments that I had kept and treasured over the years, along with my brand-new Christmas-decorated towels, pot holders, etc., out of the house that night. And to do so would definitely be going against my own desires.

We had a friend at the time living with us, so that night as I shared what I had just discovered and what I was convinced to do, she wisely advised me to check with my husband first. Kevin was on the road hauling mail for the post office, and I called him on his break. I fully expected him to say, "Wait until I get home and let's think about this." But to my surprise, Kevin said, "Do whatever you believe is right." Thinking that he didn't fully understand me, I again told him, "Doing what I am being instructed to do means getting rid of everything related to Christmas, including all our decorations and family keepsakes." I even had to get rid of his little family tree that we both loved, the one that we had been putting up and decorating every year. He had grown up with that tree—it was special. Even still, Kevin had not a hint of hesitation or questioning in his voice when he replied, "Do what you need to do." So I did, that very night.

Not once have we regretted our obedience, even through the unforeseen trials we were about to face with friends and family. We were blindsided by many of their reactions. We naively thought they would see what we were seeing while looking into the origin of Christmas traditions for themselves. We thought they would trust this discovery, or at the very least, respect what we knew our Heavenly Father was telling us to do. One of the thoughts I had back then was: *How can such a simple act of obedience on our part stir up so much trouble and misunderstanding among some of the people who have been so close to us and with whom we have worked alongside and loved for so long?*

Through all of this, we were grateful that my mother took the time to listen, read, and pray before she made the decision that she too would no longer celebrate this holiday. I attribute much of her ability in weighing facts to the leading of her Heavenly Father, whom she had learned to rely upon through a very difficult childhood. Mom's ability to think through information was also helped by her thirty years in science and teaching biology. She naturally had a more analytical mind that wasn't easily led by personal desires and feelings. Our decision was hard on all of us, but we have never turned back.

Then we had an even greater surprise and blessing that we did not see coming that followed this act of obedience concerning our removal of the Christmas tradition from our lives. We began to see more truth and have a greater understanding of the Scriptures than we had ever known in all our years of study and teaching His Word. The journey that ensued over these past few years has been intense, humbling, miraculous, difficult, and inspiring, though it came with more than a fair share of persecutions. It has been victorious, challenging, and revealing as we really began to walk closer than ever before with our Heavenly Father and His Son.

Throughout this time of insight and change, we have tried reaching our family, friends, and community in several different ways, from face-to-face meetings to writing letters. And as we intently studied and learned, by spending many more hours in His Word each day and each week than ever before in our lives, our hunger to share His truths continued to grow. Having experienced what it is like to try to share a treasured discovery with those closest to us and finding they want nothing to do with it, we decided to place anonymous, simple, challenging truths and Scripture studies in the classified section of our local newspaper. Sometimes the ads were daily, and sometimes they were weekly. We prayed someone would question the newspaper office as we asked their staff if they would take the name and number of anyone who wanted to leave their contact information for us.

There were only two people who left their name and number. One was a wheelchair-bound disabled nurse who had discovered the ads and wanted all the back issues. I copied them and mailed them to her. Another was an older gentleman and his wife who wanted to meet with us and discuss what they had personally been discovering about the Sabbath as well as other truths. We met and became friends, often studying together in our home on the Sabbath. The husband recently passed away, and we were so blessed to have known him.

Receiving only these two inquiries could have easily been discouraging, yet we realized we didn't need to see the results of our labors. Just knowing we had to be obedient in diligently learning and then sharing, in whatever capacity our Heavenly Father was leading us, was enough. Nevertheless, the many hours of studying and researching the Scriptures for those newspaper ads was growing us and grounding us even more in His truth.

As time passed, we became convinced of the need to write letters of admonishment to each of our local pastors. Again we received minimal response, but that's okay, because it's all in His timing, not ours.

So over these past few years, Kevin, Mom, and I have been intently reading, questioning, discussing, and learning to apply His Words to our daily walk in ways we had never imagined. We continued to study, individually and with each other, as well as with a handful of others who have also been discovering the same truths.

It's exciting to think that you, the reader, through these writings, could also be inspired, encouraged, and challenged for your forever future and for His kingdom! In the following chapters, your faith will be challenged. And we pray you are strengthened in truth as we were. It is time for the lies to be exposed by His Word. And know that in laying down your life for His sake, you will get it back again, stronger and more grounded, as you continue to humbly walk with your Maker.

Micah 6:8 tells what is required of *all* mankind, of how we are to act justly, love mercy, and to walk humbly with Him. To me, this verse sums up the whole reason we were created, which is a beautiful picture of the destiny He meant for each of us of walking with our Maker side by side in His way, His truth.

So now I ask the question "What if you found out Christmas is pagan?" Will knowing the facts make a difference in your life?

The next truth we discovered is…

CHAPTER 2

*What if you found out our Father commands
everyone to honor the Sabbath on the seventh day?*

A S I SAID BEFORE, WE never expected to find more
truth, nor did we have any idea it would impact us in
such a profound manner when we discovered the truth
about Christmas. But truth builds upon truth, and Scripture defines Scripture, the same as one lie builds upon another lie. So as
we discovered one truth that exposed a lie, it appeared there were
more truths to come.

Since most churches observe Sunday as their day of rest and
worship, many people assume that Sunday is the Sabbath. My
sweet daddy had wanted to honor the Sabbath, which he'd truly
believed was on Sunday. While I was growing up, he didn't allow our household to shop or go out to eat on Sunday. We went
to Sunday school and church services, came home for lunch,
took an afternoon nap (that I hated), and returned to church again
for evening "training union" and another service. He'd loved his
Heavenly Father and his Savior with all his heart and would not
conform to the ways of the world of working, shopping, or going out for any other worldly activities on what he thought was
the Sabbath. And these beliefs were shared by my mother and
bestowed upon me as well.

I had always known the command to honor the Sabbath is

one of the Ten Commandments, yet I had never questioned from childhood until recently if the way I had been taught to obey this command was correct.

I researched the meaning of the Sabbath and its history and started looking at the many verses in Scripture that speak of the Sabbath and its *rest* from Genesis to Revelation, and it was like discovering the Sabbath for the very first time. The disparity between different faith systems surrounding which day of the week, when that day begins/ends, and even whether a Sabbath should still be observed at all took me by surprise.

First, in simply looking at Genesis 2:2-3, a most convincing fact that the Sabbath was set up for *all* mankind is that our Creator started this institution of His Sabbath rest at the beginning of creation. This was long before it was given to the Israelites in the wilderness. Scripture says He sanctified the seventh day, set it apart from the other six days, and blessed it.

Then in the New Testament we found that the writer of Hebrews reiterates that our Creator rested from all His works on the seventh day in Hebrews 4:4. I find this interesting when considering that this statement about our Creator resting on the seventh day is sandwiched between the words "if they shall enter into My rest" in both verses 3 and 5. Why? And notice too how the words "if they shall enter into My rest" are stated twice. Anytime you see repetition like this in Scripture, we need to pay close attention as this usually means a strong emphasis, warning, or insight is being given. Why is the seventh-day rest that was instituted at the beginning of creation, recorded in Genesis 2:2-3, even brought up again in the New Testament written so many years later?

As you follow along in your copy of the Word, read these verses of Hebrews 4:1-11 and notice in verse 9 that the writer speaks of a "Sabbath-keeping" for the Father's people. This particular usage of the Greek word "*sabbatismos*" means a sabbath rest, according to Strong's Concordance.[2]

Now look back a few verses to Hebrews 3:18 where you see this same discussion of "entering into His rest." What question is the writer asking? Who does our Maker swear will *not* enter into His rest? Does it say that those who do not believe, who don't have faith will not enter? Or does it say that those who do not *obey* will not enter?

As I studied this passage, my question was, "Obey what?"

I dug deeper and went back to Psalm 95:11 that our Father similarly says: "As I swore in My wrath, 'if they shall enter into my rest....'" Let's back up several verses to include this statement:

> Do not harden your heart as in Meribah, And as in the day of Massah in the wilderness, when your fathers tried Me, have proved Me, though they saw My work. For forty years I was grieved with that generation, and said, 'They are a people who go astray in their hearts, and they do not know My ways.' As I swore in My wrath, 'if they shall enter into my rest...' (Psalm 95:8-11 ISR[3])

This Psalmist is referring to Exodus 17:1-7 where the Father became very angry with the grumbling and stubborn hearts of His people in the wilderness. I thought, *what can we learn from all of this? Are we not like a people wandering in the wilderness of this world? Would our Creator not get upset with us too when our hearts go astray, away from Him and His ways? Isn't this the proving ground to see who He is going to let enter into His rest, into that promised land we are all looking to enter?*

---

2   Strong's Concordance, Greek: 4520. σαββατισμός, οῦ, ὁ (*sabbatismos*) a sabbath rest – **https://biblehub.com/greek/4520.htm**

3   *The Scriptures* published by the Institute for Scripture Research (2009)

Well, if His ways include trusting Him, knowing His teachings, and following them, and these teachings include His Sabbath, then I think the writer of Hebrews is trying to tell us that the Sabbath is still relevant and not only relevant but vital! Otherwise, why would he bring it up in such a manner and with such emphasis in the New Testament?

Back to the Old Testament. We also found that the Sabbath was commanded to be followed *before* it was written down on tablets and given to Moses on Mount Sinai as you look at Exodus 16:23-30 after the Israelites had just been introduced to the Father's provision of manna. He instructed them to gather it for six days, but on the seventh day there would be a Sabbath and no gathering was to be done. The sixth day was a *preparation day* for the upcoming Sabbath rest, so they were told to gather twice as much manna and to prepare it. Notice this was a time in the wilderness *before* the giving of the Ten Commandments that also included His instructions for keeping His Sabbath day set apart from the other six days (Exodus 20:8-11). We started to see these truths for the first time as we searched the Scriptures and began to obey.

My research caused more questions to arise. Even though I'd been taught to observe the Sabbath, I was learning so much more than I'd ever known before and I was becoming more and more eager for a deeper, richer understanding of His Word. I remembered that there had been a sweet couple who came to survey Mom and Dad's property some three years earlier and mentioned something about the Sabbath. They had also talked about what sounded to me like *Jewish holidays.* And at the time I had listened politely but knew I wasn't interested in those holidays as I was content right where I was in my serving and worship on Sundays, doing what I had always known. Now I was hungry for answers and had lots of questions, so I contacted them. We met at his landscaping office and started pouring over Scriptures. I found out that they hosted a small gathering at their ranch each Sabbath, where we were invited to come. Mom and I met and studied the Word in their home for several Saturdays while Kevin was still working most weekends. Here we met others who were also trying to walk His Word by guarding our Creator's Sabbath that He blessed and designated to be on the seventh day of the week (Saturday). And Kevin, Mom, and I found that we were not alone in the same discovery of the paganism of Christmas either. This surprised us as we thought we were the only ones anywhere around who had discovered this.

As we began to look at Scriptures with fresh eyes, we started to question why the doctrines we had been taught (and had then in turn taught others, especially to teens and children) did not seem to fit what His Word was actually saying. I took many notes, studied on my own at home, and asked the same questions over and over again, trying to make sense of why the things I had grown up believing did not seem to match His Word in this most basic of His commands.

It took time. I continued to teach, serve, and attend services on Sundays with my little Pentecostal church family of nearly eleven years. Being very committed to the pre-K children, I continued to help my daughter and son-in-law in their children's ministry as well. Kevin was still working most weekends delivering mail and could not attend church services very often. And he wasn't so sure about the Sabbath actually being on Saturday.

For about six months, I continued to serve in that little church while investigating and praying about this seventh-day Sabbath discovery. I thought maybe I was supposed to stay in attendance on Sunday at our present church home and at the same time learn how to honor the Sabbath on the seventh day (Saturday) in order to share with others what was being revealed to me. I have never felt it was right to casually leave a church home. It was a commitment we had made, and we knew we had been led there some eleven years earlier. I was happy serving right where I was. I didn't leave my first church (the Baptist church) that I had grown up in until nearly forty years later, and I wasn't going to leave this little Pentecostal church that easily, either!

Growing up, I became a member of my Baptist church in Stephenville from the time I professed my faith at a tent revival at the age of five. I remember they made me wait until I was six to be baptized, to make sure I understood what I was professing. Kevin and I were married in that church. It was where we were committed to serving, learning, and watching our children make their professions of faith and follow in baptism. We loved our church family, and it wasn't until about the year 2000 that we were led to attend our oldest daughter and son-in-law's little Pentecostal church. At the time, we were going through a difficult period in our family when, on Father's Day, our son-in-law invited us to attend his church services. That little church family, unknowingly, ministered to us. They soothed the pain we were feeling from the very first time we walked through the doors. Kevin even surprised me by saying after that first service, which was very "Pentecostal" in nature, he could see himself returning to worship services there. So we continued to visit for several months.

After this time, we met with our minister at the Baptist church to let him know we were being led to another church. We shared that we were not unhappy but knew after about six months that we were being led to move our membership. He was kind and understanding, stating that he would miss us. We then stayed at that little Pentecostal church for approximately eleven years—healing, growing, worshiping, and serving.

Looking back, we could see there were times when we would wrestle for several months before making a major move in our lives. And then there were other times when we knew for sure we had been instructed to act right then. So, for several months, Mom and I continued to study and worship with that small home group on Saturdays as I continued to teach and help in the children's ministry at the Pentecostal church on Sundays. The small Sabbath group in no way condemned us for staying with our church family. They patiently showed us how to study and answer Scripture with Scripture.

I know our Heavenly Father knows exactly how to get our attention and teach each one of us. He is so patient, knowing that we are frail.

> For he knoweth our frame; he remembereth that we
> *are* dust. (Psalm 103:14 KJV)

We were learning to humble our flesh (to put to death our own desires) as we learned the fear of our Maker, seeing that humility and the fear of our Heavenly Father go hand in hand, and we dared not go against Him. (See Proverbs 22:4)

During all of this, Kevin did have occasion to attend church on Sunday as well as check out the small home group on the Sabbath. We were still searching whether we should continue worshipping at the Pentecostal church when a major turning point came in a most unexpected way from within the ministry of our own Pentecostal family. We were invited to a new out-reach called "Monday Night Chapel." Mom, Kevin, and I went the very week we were invited. Before the preaching started, and during the worship music, Mom and I went to the restroom. Then we decided to sit in the kitchen for a while, as Mom felt the music was a little loud for her ears. As we waited, she grew tired and was ready to go home.

So we waited for Kevin to come check on us and take us home. I had had to encourage him to come with us that night, to try this new chapel ministry, and I was sure he would have no problem leaving early. Well, that didn't happen. We waited and waited. Mom lay her head on the long dining table and rested. I don't know why I didn't just go and get Kevin. After about an hour, he came into the kitchen as the service ended and wanted to know why we hadn't come back. I explained.

After we got Mother home, he pulled out a handout we had received when we first entered the service. The speaker that night, a strong, very vocal female leader, had led the teaching. Kevin explained that as she began to read from Scriptures, it didn't quite match the exact chapter that was on the handout. He was intrigued as to why she'd read from and preached about the blessings and curses in Deuteronomy 28 instead.

From that night on, and for months, Kevin could not stop reading and rereading Deuteronomy 28 as well as its surrounding chapters. I had never before seen him in his copy of the Word this much, on a daily basis, sometimes several times a day. It was as if he were on a personal mission. I found him reading in his copy of the Word in the mornings with his cup of coffee instead of reading the newspaper, and in the evenings before bed, he was reading again. This was so unusual in our marriage because it was usually me who initiated the reading and discussion of Scripture. I had prayed for years for a husband who would be the spiritual leader of our home, and it seemed as if my prayers were being answered! We grew closer than we had ever been before, as he was now leading me and wanting to discuss everything that was being revealed to him.

Some of our thoughts were: "Why would this strong woman of faith be so adamant in her preaching that night concerning the blessings and curses, in this day and time? Weren't these warnings of obedience that were given to the Israelites, *for them*, and not literally for us? Isn't it a popular belief that the Old Testament was for 'back then' and the New Testament is for 'today'?"

Not long after this we realized we had to make a choice between guarding the Sabbath on the seventh day or continuing to treat Sunday as the Sabbath. But there was one more correction that our Heavenly Father had to clear up before we could totally commit to His Sabbath of rest. Kevin was still working on that day, as well as working on the other commanded annual Sabbaths (feast days) we were learning about in Leviticus 23.

Both Kevin and I had been raised by hardworking parents with very strong ethics who had especially emphasized that men should provide for their families. And Kevin was one of the hardest-working and most loyal employees I had ever seen. That was one of the reasons I married him. I saw him work even when he felt bad or was tired from staying out at night, when we were dating and first married. So to put his job on the line by telling his bosses he needed to honor the seventh-day Sabbath, as well as the other annual Sabbaths, was almost unthinkable. He had been hauling mail for this trucking company that subcontracted with the postal system, often working seven days a week, for fifteen years. Kevin rarely took time off even for holidays! So Kevin wrestled between his commitment to his job and blindly obeying his Heavenly Father. For several months he prayed, read, and reread his Scriptures. Finally, one day, he approached his supervisor with his ID and access badge in hand, ready to turn it in and resign should they refuse his request for the days he was now asking off, which were every Saturday as well as the annual feast days. He had no other jobs lined up and was completely trusting that his Heavenly Father would provide. He bravely told his supervisors he was convinced of the need to follow the commands in the Scriptures concerning these days. He later relayed that he had said to them, "If you cannot give me these days off, then here's my badge." This was such a leap of faith for my loyal, hardworking husband. This act of obedience was truly laying down his life (his livelihood) and going against his own nature in order to completely trust in his Heavenly Father's words!

And to Kevin's amazement, his supervisor had said, "We

will work with you. Tell us the days you will need off. We have another driver who is doing the same thing."

Kevin had never expected this response! He discovered that all he had to do was be willing to lose his job and our financial security, which is one of the hardest things any hardworking responsible man could ever do! Now he was able to keep his job and honor his Heavenly Father's Sabbaths at the same time! But we know for many who discover this same truth, who take this same step of faith, the consequences are very often not the same but can result in the loss of their job. Sincere followers will (and do) suffer for doing good and are called "blessed" when they persevere in following our Father's Word:

> But if you should suffer for righteousness' sake, you will be blessed. Have no fear of them, nor be troubled. (1 Peter 3:14 ESV)

> Not only that, but we rejoice in our sufferings, knowing that suffering produces endurance, (Romans 5:3 ESV)

We are commanded to trust our Maker with all our heart and to not lean on our own understanding, but in all our ways, we are to acknowledge Him and He will direct our paths. (See Proverbs 3:5-6) I like how the Contemporary English Version translates these verses: "Always let him lead you, and he will clear the road for you to follow."

The words of several old hymns I grew up with still ring true: "Though none go with me, still I will follow" and "Not a burden we bear, not a sorrow we share, but to all he doth richly repay. While we do His good will, He abides with us still, and with all who will trust and obey. Trust and obey, for there's no other way."[4]

Soon after this miracle with Kevin's job, we stopped serving

---

4   **https://hymnary.org/hymn/TTvirt/168**

and attending worship services at the little Pentecostal church. We knew we needed to meet with our pastor but were waiting for the right words and timing. At the prompting of our concerned daughter, we made the appointment and started praying for Scripture to share with him. We respected him as a much more studied leader of the church and the Word than we were. I was sure he knew all the verses concerning the Sabbath that we knew. So we prayed for a specific and personal confirmation in the Scriptures to share with him as to why we would take such a turn in our spiritual walk.

In my searching of Scriptures, I often randomly opened His Word and scanned the pages to see what my Heavenly Father had to tell me. So that is what I did, and my eyes landed on Deuteronomy 29 and Exodus 19:12. As I began to read in Deuteronomy 29 from verse 1 to verse 4, it became clear what we needed to share, as this passage spoke of a time that our Father does not give eyes to see, ears to hear, or a heart to know certain things until *His timing*.

Our Heavenly Father *waits* to reveal certain truths to His people. He then gives us the ability to understand and see things that were right in front of us the whole time, right before our eyes, but in His timing.

So when we met with our pastor, we shared these Scriptures and related that even today we are not given eyes to see, ears to hear, or a heart to know until He has us in the place and timing that is perfect in His plan for us. Concerning the Sabbath not being on Sunday and man's traditional holidays that we were now letting go of in our lives, we really wanted to share with him why we believed these truths were coming to light for us *now*. So I said, "Pastor, I really believe that our Heavenly Father is showing us how to get our garments clean." And then these words came out of my mouth concerning the holidays we were letting go of, "I don't think we can make something pagan, holy." I didn't fully understand the gravity of these last words until much later in our walk. I also wanted him to know that I believed these revelations were not even for my dad to know, in his time of life on this Earth. This pastor had known my dad years earlier as a student on the Tarleton campus during the time when my dad had been the director of the Baptist Student Union. And I believed our pastor also held my dad, as I did, to have been one of the humblest men he had ever known. Daddy truly loved and lived everything His Heavenly Father showed him. He ministered to many people in our small town—in particular, two older men who struggled daily with alcohol addiction and had lost everything because of it. My humble, serving dad faithfully fed, housed, and even cleaned after they had been sick, while witnessing to them, praying for them, and advocating for them with their families and landlords. My dad believed in living his faith no matter what anyone else thought of him or how lowly the job. I also remember several times, in the eleven years we were under the leadership of this Pentecostal pastor, his servant's heart had also reminded me of my dad.

As we talked, Kevin and I shared the other verse I had found:

> But you shall set boundaries for the people all around, saying "Beware that you do not go up on the mountain or touch the border of it; whoever touches the mountain shall surely be put to death. (Exodus 19:12 NASB)

I told of our awe at what had appeared to be an extremely bold and harsh command that the Father gave Moses to give to the children of Israel. When I'd found this verse earlier that week, I could not believe how extreme my Heavenly Father sounded when He told the Israelites not to even touch the mountain or they would die. I didn't remember ever reading or studying that verse before!

Kevin and I were beginning to realize that it doesn't matter whether we like what our Heavenly Father says or even fully understand why He is giving an instruction. If He says don't touch it, we don't touch it! In other words, if the Creator of the heavens and the Earth, and all that is in them—the most powerful force in the universe—gives mankind instruction, we too would be wise to heed His words whether we understand why or not, and whether we like His command or not. Who are we to doubt His knowledge and love for us? If it is within our power to heed His instructions and at the same time not break any of the laws of the land that we are living in, then shouldn't we obey Him? And shouldn't we constantly strive to find out what pleases Him? It's all too easy to talk ourselves out of obeying His commands with thoughts like, "This isn't the way I was raised," "They never taught me this in church," "I could lose everything," "What will people think," or even "That's not what this means to *me*." We've been conditioned to believe and think from our human perspective and not from our Maker's, especially when His perspective and what pleases Him goes against our own thoughts, desires, customs, and even the doctrines we've been taught. Yet it's vital to learn how to discern whether it is our flesh or our Heavenly Father's leading as we navigate through this life.

Here's the secret. It is a red flag for me when I hear my flesh saying, "It's so much easier not to change my actions, rather than to go against what I'd really like to do." If we are being led to act contrary to our own fleshly desires, *and* it is in accordance with the words of our Heavenly Father and His Son, then we know it is the leading of our Heavenly Father's Spirit. It's kind of like a spiritual litmus test. Remember our Messiah's words telling us that what He instructs is narrow and set apart from what everyone else is doing? Satan deceivingly whispers, "If it was right, more people would see it and be doing it," which totally goes against the following truth:

Enter by the narrow gate. For the gate is wide and the

way is easy that leads to destruction, and those who
enter by it are many. (Matthew 7:13-14 ESV)

Someone recently asked, "What does 'set apart' mean?" My
first thought is to say, "Set apart means to be set apart unto righteousness from the ways of this world, to *not* follow the crowd
nor the paths that the world promotes."

There is a way *that seems* right to a man, but its end
is the way of death. (Proverbs 14:12 NKJV)

I want to take a moment here to deviate from our main discussion of leading up to the specifics of our Sabbath research
to include a couple of very important truths I learned from the
time we spent with this very special pastor at the little Pentecostal church. The first truth was that we are to pray as our Messiah taught us to pray, to our Heavenly Father, and to begin our
prayers to the Father in the Son's name. We still pray to this day
in this same manner as we say, "Father, in the name of…"

And the second truth our pastor taught us, which at first I
had not been able to believe what I heard him say during that
particular sermon, is that we could lose our salvation. At least
that's what I'd thought I heard him say. So I made an appointment to meet with him that very week. I was going to make sure
I was hearing him right, because in my Baptist upbringing, I had
been taught (and had in turn witnessed to strangers during a Baptist outreach called Evangelism Explosion) that once you were
saved, you were always saved. We were taught to back this belief
with the verse that talked about no one being able to snatch you
out of the Father's hand.

If what I was then hearing from this pastor was true, my
whole security in my salvation seemed in jeopardy. As my pastor
and I sat down, he explained that you cannot "lose" your salvation, but you *can* knowingly and *deliberately* walk away from it.
He gave the analogy, "If you were to walk into my office and lay
your keys down but didn't realize you had laid them down, that's

called losing them. But if you came into my office and *purpose-fully, deliberately* left them on my desk and walked away from them, that action is *knowingly walking away*. And this is true of our salvation, that *we can knowingly and deliberately walk away from it.*" I didn't want to believe this! But it did begin to make sense, and it did line up with Scriptures. Look at Hebrews 6:4-6 and 10:26-29. These truths continue to be affirmed over and over again throughout all the Scriptures, from the Old to the New Testament. I will expand further on these verses in Hebrews in later chapters in this book.

In the following months after leaving the little Pentecostal church and having met with our pastor to say "goodbye," we continued our quest to learn more and more about this institution called "the Sabbath." As much as Kevin and I had taught the creation story to children, there was something else we hadn't realized in Genesis chapter 1. What does it say about when a day starts? Doesn't it say over and over again, "So the evening and morning were…"? For the first time, we saw that our Heavenly Father defines the beginning of a day, not at midnight, but at sundown! A day begins at sundown in the evening. So, the seventh day (the Sabbath) begins at sundown on the sixth day. Another Scripture that clarifies when a day starts is Leviticus 23:27 and 32 for the observance of the Day of Atonement. Our Father wanted to make sure there is no mistake as to what the tenth day of the seventh month is and that it starts on the evening of the ninth day.

Knowing these facts of when a day starts and ends, we now understand so much more of what was happening, not only in the lives of the ancient Israelites but also in the lives of our Messiah and His followers, especially surrounding His death, burial, and resurrection as recorded in the New Testament.

How important was and is the Sabbath to our Creator? Wouldn't He make it very clear if He were going to change this most important of His institutions? Who claims to have changed the Sabbath from the seventh day to the first day? If you do an internet search for "Cardinal Gibbons Sabbath Day" you will find several websites describing and containing articles that he personally wrote in the *Catholic Mirror* as well as in the book he authored called *Faith of Our Fathers*. Of a special note is the website and pamphlet entitled Rome's Challenge.[5] These writings connect the change from worship on Saturday directly to the Roman Catholic Church, and then connecting the Protestant churches to the same practice as they follow the leadership of the Roman Catholic authorities.

Cardinal Gibbons stated that nowhere in all of Scripture from Genesis to Revelation can it be found that the Sabbath was ever changed from the seventh day to the first day. The Catholic Church confirms this over and over when it declares that *she* has the sole power and the right to change the day of worship from the Sabbath to Sunday.

He wrote in a signed letter in the *Catholic Mirror,* official publication of James, Cardinal Gibbons, September 23, 1893:

> Is Saturday the seventh day according to the Bible and the Ten Commandments? I answer yes. Is Sunday the first day of the week, and did the Church change the seventh day—Saturday—for Sunday, the first day? I answer yes. Did Christ change the day? I answer no!

It is easy to research other declarations by both Catholic and Protestant leaders with the same proclamations concerning the Sabbath being on the seventh day. Here are just a couple of examples of well-respected Protestant leaders who declared that the Sabbath was never abolished or changed:

Baptist minister Dr. Edward T. Hiscox, in a paper read before

---

5   https://romeschallenge.com/

a New York ministers' conference, November 13, 1893, as reported in the *New York Examiner*, November 16, 1893:

> "There was and is a commandment to keep holy the Sabbath day, but that Sabbath day was not Sunday. It will be said, however, and with some show of triumph, that the Sabbath was transferred from the seventh to the first day of the week... Where can the record of such a transaction be found? Not in the New Testament, absolutely not. To me it seems unaccountable that Jesus, during three years' intercourse with His disciples, often conversing with them upon the Sabbath question ... never alluded to any transference of the day; also, that during forty days of His resurrection life, no such thing was intimated. Of course, I quite well know that Sunday did come into use in early Christian history ... But what a pity it comes branded with the mark of paganism and christened with the name of the sun god, adopted and sanctioned by the papal apostasy, and bequeathed as a sacred legacy to Protestantism!"

Dwight L. Moody, in *Weighed and Wanting*, pp. 47-48:

> "The sabbath was binding in Eden, and it has been in force ever since. This fourth commandment begins with the word "remember," showing that the sabbath already existed when God wrote the law on the tables of stone at Sinai. How can men claim that this one commandment has been done away with when they will admit that the other nine are still binding?"

You can also research where the pope stands on this issue, as well as the present teachings of the Catholic Church. This present pope, Francis, refers to the Sabbath as the "Jewish Sabbath," making it sound like the Sabbath is and always was for the Jews as opposed to Sunday being the new institution for Christians. However, in looking at Genesis chapter 2, we see that the Sabbath was instituted long before there was a distinction between Jew and Gentile and long before it was given to "the Jews" on Mount Sinai. And Mark 2:27-28 says the Sabbath was made for man. Where in this verse does it say that the Sabbath was made exclusively for the Jews?

And historical records also note that Constantine as well as the Council of Laodicea both declared laws to change worship from Saturday to Sunday. Men changed a divine law of our Creator. This is what we have inherited.

Another thought that would further the evidence concerning the Sabbath being on the seventh day came to me as I wondered if there was any evidence that the seventh day of the week is also (and continues to be) called the Sabbath in other cultures and languages. Well, when I did an internet search simply for "seventh day of the week in other languages," I found that not only is the seventh day called "*yom sabat*" in Hebrew, but in French it is called "*samedi*," meaning day of the Sabbath. In Italian it is *sabato*, in Latin it is *sabbatum*, in Polish *sobota*, in Portuguese and Spanish it is *sabado*, and so on, in several other languages—all of which means "Sabbath."

And on the website omniglot.com (the online encyclopedia of writing systems and languages), I found that some other languages, besides the English language, also use the pagan "Saturn" or "Saturday" to describe the seventh day. For example, in German, *Samstag* means Saturn day, and in Afrikaans, *Saterdag* means Saturn's day.

It was also very interesting to see that every name of the other six days of our week is associated with some form of pagan deity or pagan worship in most languages. Monday is associated with the moon day in French, Tuesday with Mars day in Irish, Wednesday with Woden's day in Afrikaans, Thursday with Thunder's (Thor's) day in German, Friday with Frige's day in Old English and Venus day in several other languages. C. J. Koster, in his book, *Come Out of Her, My People*, cites the same pagan connection to the names of the days of the week that the English language uses as well. And doesn't Scripture tell us literally not to mention the names of other deities, to not let them be heard on our lips?

After reading the book *Come Out of Her, My People* and doing my own research into the etymology of the names of the days of the week and months of the year, I realized just how much our beliefs and even our language are rooted in Greek and Roman pagan worship and mythology. Another reference I found called "Ancient Origins" gives the history of names we inherited and so commonly use for each day of the week: **https://www.ancient-origins.net/myths-legends/pagan-gods-and-naming-days-001037**. Although I do not agree with many of the other articles on this website, especially having to do with evolution and the dating of how old the Earth is thought to be, I did find this particular article concerning the origin of the names we commonly use to be unbiased and a good source of history on this subject.

And so began so much correction in how Kevin, Mom, and I began to talk. We figured that if we are faithful in the smaller details of life, especially in our language, we should be trustworthy in the bigger details of life. Before you conclude that the "cleaning up" of so much of our everyday speech is absurd, it would be good to stop and think about the following verses:

> But I tell you that *for* every careless word that people speak, they will give an account of it on *the* day of judgment. For by your words you will be justified, and by your words you will be condemned. (Matthew 12:36-37 NASB)

One who guards his mouth and his tongue, guards his soul from troubles. (Proverbs 21:23 NASB)

It still isn't easy to stop using the names of other deities, as daily, we use these words to communicate concerning the days of the week and the months of the year. Taming the tongue is definitely a challenge!

Now concerning everything which I have said to you, be careful; and do not mention the name of other gods, nor let *them* be heard from your mouth. (Exodus 23:13 NASB)

And in our realizing that the days of the week are names of other deities that were worshiped, in writing this book, I thought about leaving out some of the letters in the complete spelling of the days of the week to emphasize that we are trying to follow our Father's commands as we speak our "every day" language. Then I thought about using the number of each day of the week rather than its name. For example, I would call Sunday "first day" and Monday "second day" and so on. But I decided this might be confusing as you read this book and decided to leave these words in their written form with their complete spelling.

If you still don't think any of this is important, I'd like to challenge you to humbly pray and keep reading His Word, especially noticing what He has to say in connection with the Sabbath. Let His Word decide whether keeping/guarding His Sabbath is important or not. Exodus 31:13-18 and Ezekiel 20:12-49 both say His Sabbaths are a sign between Him and His people to set them apart.

And I also gave them my Sabbaths, to be a sign

between them and Me, to know that I am יהוה who
sets them apart. (Ezekiel 20:12 ISR[6])

We have a friend who asked this question: "If the seventh-
day worship is a sign or mark of the Father upon His people,
whose sign or mark is the first-day worship?"

That is a profound question.

When you research the word "sign" in *Strong's Exhaustive
Concordance,* in Hebrew it means "a mark, miracle, or ensign."
If indeed keeping His Sabbaths is this important—if it is a sign
or a mark between the Creator and His people—then I want to
be in that set-apart group of people that He calls "His"! And can
you see that during the end times of the Tribulation, when the
anti-messiah is marking his people, that for those who guard the
Sabbath, this could very well have something to do with being
marked or even sealed by our Heavenly Father? I discuss the
anti-messiah and his mark in more detail in the coming chapters.

In Hebrews 10:25, its writer says not to forsake the gathering
together of the believers (saints). I was taught this verse meant,
"Be sure to attend church on Sunday." Now I know Paul never
meant that!

Our Messiah, and even Paul after the Messiah died, kept the
Sabbath and the feast days as commandments that were included
within the Law. Further note that in His Word, our Creator gives
the consequences for profaning His Sabbaths. The words "gave
them up" in Ezekiel 20:25 remind me of the same words "gave
them up" in Romans 1:24. (I hate hearing those words!) And as
you read the rest of Ezekiel Chapter 20, does it not look like the
future gathering of His people? It talks about a purging of rebels,
a fire that all flesh shall see, and it states that He has kindled that
fire, which is unquenchable.

---

6   I am using the ISR translation here because of its Hebrew rendering
of the Father's name. More will be explained in the next chapter concerning
the Father and Son's names.

There are many warnings as well as promises in His Word concerning the Sabbath. We've already discussed at the beginning of this chapter, the warning about not getting to enter His rest in Hebrews chapter 4. Now look at this promise in Isaiah chapter 58. I was very familiar with the beginning verses, especially in verses 6-7 below, having heard numerous sermons on this subject.

> Is this not the fast that I have chosen: to loosen the tight cords of wrongness, to undo the bands of the yoke, to exempt the oppressed, and to break off every yoke? Is it not to share your bread with the hungry, and that you bring to your house the poor who are cast out; when you see the naked, and cover him, and not hide yourself from your own flesh? (Isaiah 58:6-7 ISR)

The prophet Isaiah continues to quote more of our Father's instructions and promises in verses 8-12, all of which sound good and noble for all believers to follow, both past and present, especially the instructions of reaching out and helping others. Yet my question today is, "Why in the very same chapter when it comes to verses 13 and 14 concerning our Father's instructions in guarding the Sabbath are we not taught to obey these instructions too?"

> If you do turn back your foot from the Sabbath, from doing your pleasure on My set-apart *day*, and shall call the Sabbath "a delight," the set-apart day of יהוה "esteemed," and shall esteem it, not doing your own ways, nor finding your own pleasure, nor speaking your own words, then you shall delight yourself in יהוה. And I shall cause you to ride on the heights of the earth, and feed you with the inheritance of Ya'aqob your father. For the mouth of יהוה has spoken! (Isaiah 58:13-14 ISR)

What happened? Could it be that if we were taught to keep the seventh-day Sabbath of resting from our work by turning back from doing our own pleasures on His set-apart day, to delight in it and esteem it, not doing our own ways, nor speaking our own words, that it would not tickle our ears nor be very popular? How would this affect the message and attendance of the churches today? Would we have to put the Sabbath before our livelihoods, our weekend work, and our weekend pleasures? What would happen to the pastors who would have the nerve to humbly stand before their congregation and say, "I was wrong"? Would their denomination or even their congregation support them in changing worship back to Saturday? What would the Roman Catholic Church say to our Protestant churches if they quit following the leadership of the "mother church" that declares Sunday as the day of rest?

Scott Hillman, a minister from the background of the Assemblies of God denomination, had the strength and humility to stand up and declare that he had been wrong. Visit **https://youtu. be/-nkJg8tPSOg** to see what happened when he approached his denominational leaders about his discovery of the truth of keeping the Sabbath on the seventh day.

Kevin, Mom, and I also observed what others were doing in keeping the Sabbath and how they carried out the intent of the Scriptures. But we were very careful to pray and compare what they were doing with what our Heavenly Father and His set-apart Spirit were teaching us through His Word. We in no way wanted to go right back into following men or their traditions! These are the questions we began to answer:

Exactly how would you go about every week, setting the seventh day apart from the other six days of the week?

What does 'set apart' mean and look like for this commanded day of rest?

What does His Word really say in the Ten Commandments

when it says, "You shall not work, you nor your son nor your daughter nor your male or female servant, nor your cattle nor the sojourner who stays with you.'"?

Here's what we learned:

First and foremost, to guard the Sabbath command, is to literally not work as you would the other six days for pay, nor cause or support anyone else working for pay.

It encompasses for us to cease and reschedule on other days our activities of shopping, eating out, garage sales, sports events, mowing the lawn, cleaning house, cooking meals, going to the movies, working, and causing others to work. We have also determined that to set His Sabbath day apart, to meet with Him and to gather with others to honor and focus on Him and His Word, we do not attend celebrations of birthdays, weddings, anniversaries, graduations, funerals, and memorials that honor our friends and loved ones. We were learning that to put Him first we prioritize our time unto Him on this day. Who of us has not scheduled work around birthday parties as well as vice versa? But to prioritize and reschedule our lives and events around guarding the Sabbath sounds very narrow and set apart from what the rest of the world is doing on the weekends. Could this "set-apartness" be exactly what our Heavenly Father wants?

Stop right here before you get too upset, especially if you are a believer who loves your Messiah. Open your Scriptures to Luke 9:59-62 and look at His statements concerning the dead and loyalty to family.

And *He* said to another, 'Follow Me,' but he said, 'Master, let me first go and bury my father.' And יהושע said to him, 'Let the dead bury their own dead, but you go and announce the reign of Elohim." And another also said, 'Master, I shall follow You, but let me first say good-bye to those in my house.' But יהושע said to him, 'No one, having put his hand to

the plough, and looking back, is fit for the reign of
Elohim.'(Luke 9:59-62 ISR[7])

How could He say that? This sounds very harsh for such a
loving Messiah. And look at His words concerning His mother
and brothers in Matthew 12:47-50. We have to admit that many
times we don't like what Scripture says. It's hard to accept the
bold and seemingly blatant statements our Messiah made, especially concerning family. His words are uncomfortable to our
flesh. They go against the way we want to live our lives, especially *who* we want to honor and put first. Is it easier to ask forgiveness of our Creator than it is to ask forgiveness of our family
and friends? If the answer is yes, it is easier to ask forgiveness
of our Heavenly Father for missing His Sabbaths, His appointed
times with Him, than it is to ask forgiveness of our friends and
family for missing their celebrations and their memorials, then
isn't this viewpoint dangerously close to placing our friends and
family above pleasing and honoring our Maker?

We began to have our eyes opened to the fact that we had
been prioritizing what we wanted to do and pleasing others first,
above loving and obeying our Heavenly Father and His Word.

After all, what does it really mean to love our Heavenly Father with *all* our heart, soul, mind, and strength and to walk in His
commands as His Son did? Are we really exempt from fulfilling
this command? I know this may sound strong, but idolatry is not
just the worship of idols but idolatry is also the act of placing
"things" first in our lives above our love and obedience to our
Creator and placing others in the position of respect and honor
that rightfully belongs to Him. How can we say we love Him
first with all our hearts, yet do what pleases us and others first?
We are either committed to Him first, or we are not.

Early on in our walk for truth, Kevin, Mother, and I knew we

---

7   Again the ISR translation is used for the Hebrew rendering of the
Messiah's name.

could not truly honor our Heavenly Father's command to guard and set His Sabbaths apart on the same day that we honored and celebrated others and their achievements. We were earnestly tested on several occasions from birthday parties to graduations. The ones we loved—but whose activities we refused to put first on the Sabbath—did not understand in the beginning.

The words of Matthew 10:34-39 concerning the division that our Savior came to bring started to hit home as we began to keep our Father's Sabbath day. We never thought we would experience His words concerning His division of families. I'd never given these verses much thought before, or really understood them, until we ended up living them. Our actions, whether we liked it or not, were beginning to set us apart. This is a truth, and its depth you cannot know until you have lived it.

The details of these tests are etched in my memory, but they will not be shared here out of respect for our family. We have forgiven them, and we pray that they have forgiven us. As stated in the beginning pages of this book, there has been much healing in our family despite the fact that we have never backed down from setting apart His Sabbaths. These trials were some of the most difficult times for us, as well as for the rest of our family. (See Chapter 4 in this book entitled "What if you found out our Messiah came to bring division, even among family members?")

We pondered these questions. Could our Heavenly Father, the Creator of the heavens and the Earth, who is the most powerful force in the universe, really ask us to give up so much? Is this what our Messiah was talking about when He said we are not worthy of Him unless we are willing to lay down our lives for His sake? Could our Maker be pulling us back from the world and its priorities in order to set us apart for His kingdom? Well, as you can see, we were finding out that following His command to guard His Sabbath according to His Son's example and the prophet Isaiah's words absolutely separates us from a lot!

A close family member commented concerning our new-found commitments to the Father, "It looks like you belong to a very elite group of people." Looking back, I now take that comment as a compliment. I do consider being part of a group of people who strive to walk "the narrow path" as our Messiah walked in His Father's way (and I pray hears the words, "And they shall be My people") as an honor and a privilege. These are some of the most beautiful and endearing words found in both the Old and New Testaments, to be called "His people." Could all that we had been learning and experiencing be what the Scriptures are talking about when they say, "Come out of her, My people"?

So if you have begun to realize that it is imperative to keep the command concerning our Maker's seventh-day Sabbath, I want to encourage you because you will be tested.

> Consider it pure joy, my brothers and sisters, whenever you face trials of many kinds, because you know that the testing of your faith produces perseverance. Let perseverance finish its work so that you may be mature and complete, not lacking anything. (James 1:2-4 NIV)

One of the blessings I've always enjoyed while growing up in church was the long tables of covered dishes with homemade casseroles, pies, salads, etc. I guess you might call me a "foodie" from a very young age. As soon as I was old enough to cook an entire meal for a group of people (about age twelve), I began serving my junior high/high school church choir, as we took turns providing a meal during our practices. I loved cooking and serving in each of my church homes over the years. Now it's the same, as we gather with other believers for the weekly seventh-day Sabbath and the annual feast days. I continue to cook, share, and especially enjoy others' recipes and covered dishes. After eating, we sing, pray for one another, read, and discuss Scripture.

These are special times (set-apart times) where we step away from the routines of our lives, to rest from the world and from our work, and to focus on things above and not on things of the Earth. These are set-apart gatherings.

We continue to personalize within our family different ways of setting His day apart as we delight in His Sabbath, which results in delighting in Him. Isaiah 58:13-14 ISR says "If you do turn back your foot from the Sabbath, from doing your pleasure on My set-apart day, and shall call the Sabbath 'a delight,' the set-apart day of יהוה esteemed, and shall esteem it, not doing your own ways, nor finding your own pleasure, nor speaking your own words, then you shall delight yourself in יהוה. And I shall cause you to ride on the heights of the earth, and feed you with the inheritance of Ya'aqob your father. For the mouth of יהוה has spoken!"

When we delight in our Father not only do we get the same inheritance He promised Jacob (the overcomer), but He then gives us the desires of our heart (Psalm 37:4). Why do you think He would give us the desires of our heart? I believe it is because we will have pursued the desire of His heart, especially in keeping His Sabbath. And our hearts will be full of the same desires as His. Do you see how serious He is about His Sabbaths? He greatly rewards those who seek His will (His heart's desire for them).

> But without belief it is impossible to please Him, for he who comes to Elohim has to believe that He is, and that He is a rewarder of those who earnestly seek Him. (Hebrews 11:6 ISR)

According to Isaiah 58:13-14, we will ride on the heights of the Earth. I like to think of this as "getting the best of everything." Think about it: who wouldn't want the best things—complete and unending love, joy and peace, protection, safety, no hunger, no worry, no stress, and so much more than we can imagine!

These times of keeping His Sabbaths (His set-apart days and appointments with Him) are so encouraging as we fellowship, learn together, and ask each other questions. Most of the people I have gathered with, in and near my hometown, use a suggested reading called the "Torah Portion." This is a cyclical schedule of reading the books of the Law from Genesis through Deuteronomy each year. In addition to these weekly readings, we read from the books of the Prophets and the New Testament.

It is good to pray about how the Father would have you carry out the intent of Isaiah 58:13-14 just as we would pray and question how we should carry out the other verses in the beginning and middle of Isaiah 58. It also helps to look at the book of Acts and the gospels to see the activities of our Messiah and his followers (including Paul) on the Sabbath and feast days. Did they gather with other believers? Did they read from the Law and Prophets and discuss the Father's kingdom?

And in learning how to honor, guard, and set apart His Sabbaths, it is important to refrain from just copying what others are doing simply because it's easier to follow them. Test everything against His Word and personally rely upon it. Here are some verses to help you get started: Genesis 2:2-3, Isaiah 58:13-14, Exodus 20:8-11, Hebrews 10:25, and 2 Timothy 2:24-25, 3:14-17, and 4:2-5. As you read through these verses, I want to encourage you to rely on prayer, His Son's examples in the gospel writings of the New Testament, and the leading of the set-apart Spirit.

According to Scripture, the keeping of His Sabbath is practical. If someone has a flat tire on the Sabbath, you help them. If you have a sick family member at home or in the hospital, you tend to them. If your neighbor has cows or livestock out, you help him round them up. If you have animals that must be watered and fed daily, you continue to care for them. We have done all these things on the Sabbath. You do not ignore the needs

of others or the needs of the ones Your Heavenly Father has entrusted to your care, as our Messiah gave example.

Desires, which are often confused with needs, should be
weighed within the wisdom of His Word. It is important to
communicate with family and friends ahead of time about what
His Word and set-apart Spirit are telling you concerning their
celebrations, commemorations, etc. His appointed times are appointments with Him, created by Him. He demands and deserves
priority not only every day, but especially on His set-apart days.
Sometimes we have to choose between pleasing Him and pleasing others.

Keeping and guarding the Sabbath is a rhythm of life: work
six days and rest on the seventh, work six days and rest on the
seventh, as our Maker designed. We all need this twenty-four-
hour break from the world mentally, spiritually, and physically.
Please know, you will miss out on what the world schedules on
the Sabbath from sundown on the sixth day to sundown on the
seventh day. We cannot stop the world's agendas. Over time, I
pray your family and friends will come to respect *Who* you put
first and even learn themselves that in loving and putting our
Heavenly Father and His Son first, it does not mean you do not
love each other as well. Do you think our Messiah loved His
mother, brothers, and sisters? Yet, *Who* did He love first with all
His heart?

My prayer continues to be that you carefully search for truth,
always with a humble, fearful heart, while being willing to lay
down *anything* your Heavenly Father reveals to you through His
Spirit and His Word, no matter what. You will likely hear the
following excuses just like we heard and once believed:

"People should worship every day of the week so it doesn't
matter which day you choose to be your Sabbath" or "Sunday is
the Lord's day on the day that He rose from the dead, and that is
why we worship on it" and so on.

Remember, our Heavenly Father and His Son did not change this most important of commandments—man did! And I know we do not have the right to change any of them. He is a very jealous power that does not like anyone changing His instructions. Here's what Isaiah the prophet recorded concerning the future:

> The earth mourns *and* fades away, the world languishes *and* fades away; the haughty people of the earth languish. The earth is also defiled under its inhabitants, because they have transgressed the laws, changed the ordinance, broken the everlasting covenant. (Isaiah 24:4-5 NKJV)

This passage shows what the future is going to be for the people who pridefully defy Him, who change and transgress His laws, His ordinances. Keep reading in Isaiah chapter 24 on into chapters 25, 26, and 27 to see a wonderfully different future of how He provides for those who humbly obey Him. And during this prophetic time of judgment, found in these chapters of Isaiah, you will also read of how He is going to tell His people to enter their rooms and shut their doors for a little while until His fury has passed.

Again, it takes a humble, teachable, fearful heart, searching for the truth and willing to let the truth change and mold it into denying the flesh and obeying the Creator. Only in this way can you carefully and prayerfully discern the information you need. In this day and time that we have been chosen to live, we need to especially think about what we are believing, and question what we have been taught, running it through the timeless test of His Word and His Spirit. And finally, we must compare His Word with what the world is believing, teaching, and doing. All the while, know that our Heavenly Father's way to walk as His Son walked will never be popular.

The keeping of the Sabbath *is setting apart* those who guard it and remains just as vital to obey as it did several thousand years ago when our Creator first instituted it at the beginning of His Creation. It is paramount for living in His will today and for entering into His rest in each of our futures. Satan, through man's actions, has changed our Father's words and we have blindly gone along with it.

Personally, I *do* wish to enter into life and rest, now and forever. I'm learning to take His instructions seriously, especially concerning the Sabbath. Just as a parent warns his child of the need to follow his instructions when he says to stay out of a busy street while playing, our Heavenly Father gave us these commands for our good always.

So now that you know the truth about the Sabbath, what will you do? Will this truth matter to you?

CHAPTER 3
What if you found out our Heavenly Father's
name isn't God and His Son's name isn't Jesus?

W HAT DIFFERENCE WOULD IT MAKE? Or would you think, *He knows I'm talking to Him. It shouldn't matter what name I use.*

Would you search to see if the words "God," "Lord," and even "Jesus Christ" are backed by Scripture and historical research as the true names of our Heavenly Father and His Son?

And if these are not their true names, how did we end up with them in our Bibles?

Well, when I did an internet search for the etymology of the word "god," I read that this word is Germanic in origin and not Hebraic at all. This word "god" is also Old English, related to the Dutch "*god*" and the German "*gott*." The article also stated that "God" is used not only by Christians for describing their Supreme Being, but also used by other monotheistic religions to describe and call upon their supreme being as well. The title "God" appears to be widely generic. However, reading and agreeing with this one article still wasn't enough to make me change how I had always called upon my Heavenly Father.

As we were studying and worshipping with our small group of friends on the Sabbath, we noticed they often used the words "Father," "Messiah," and "Yahuweh" or "Yahweh" for God, and

"Yahushua" or "Yahshua" instead of Jesus. I asked them why they didn't use the common names of God, Jesus, Christ, and Lord. Their response was that these are not their true names, and to the best of their understanding, they believed these names were never endorsed by our Creator, His Son, or the disciples.

Still, I wasn't going to change what I had always done in calling on and talking about my Heavenly Father and His Son based on what other people say and do. I needed more evidence. "Yahuweh" for "God," and "Yahushua" for Jesus were still foreign to Kevin's, Mom's, and my ears and speech. This wasn't what we had been taught.

We were drawn to further examine the words given to the prophet in Jeremiah. This prophecy states that in a day of trouble (distress), the Gentiles (nations) will come to the Almighty and say, as recorded in Jeremiah:

> Surely our fathers have inherited lies, worthlessness, and unprofitable *things*. Will a man make gods for himself, which are not gods? Therefore behold, I will this once cause them to know, I will cause them to know My hand and My might; and they shall know that My name *is* the Lord. (Jeremiah16:19b-21 NKJV)

In the above verse, how can His name be "the LORD" in the Old Testament and His Son's name be "the Lord" with only the "L" being in caps in the New Testament? When you stop and think about this, it doesn't make any sense. Additionally, Jeremiah's prophecy seems to imply that our Creator's name would be lost and then found. I was beginning to doubt that our Heavenly Father, being so adamant in Jeremiah 16:19-21 about the Gentiles knowing the truth of who He really is and what He really demands concerning His name, idol worship, inherited lies, and futility, would use such a generic title as "the LORD" for His Name.

Therefore My people shall know My name; therefore *they shall know* in that day that I *am* He who speaks: "Behold, *it is* I." (Isaiah 52:6 NKJV)

The writer of the following Proverb even asks the question:

Who has ascended into heaven, or descended? Who has gathered the wind in His fists? Who has bound the waters in a garment? Who has established all the ends of the earth? What *is* His name, and What *is* His Son's name, if you know? (Proverbs 30:4 NKJV)

You may still think, "What difference does it make what names we use as long as we are sincere?"

Well, I think it makes a great deal of difference to our Creator and to His Son, as noted in these Scripture references. I found one of the best ways to research what our Heavenly Father and His Son have to say about their names is with my *Strong's Concordance* that had been collecting dust on the bookshelf for years. I purchased it while working at a Christian bookstore in 2004. So for me to get a more comprehensive understanding of a particular subject or word, for example the word "name," I began to research that key word and see all its different references in both the Old and New Testaments. It is amazing what a broad picture you can get in doing word searches with a *Strong's Concordance*!

These are two of the verses I found that really opened my eyes concerning their names:

…This is My Name forever, and this is My remembrance to all generations. (Exodus 3:15b ISR):

If you do not listen, and if you do not take it to heart to give honor to My name,' says the LORD of armies, 'then I will send the curse upon you, and I will curse your blessings; and indeed, I have cursed them *already*, because you are not taking *it* to heart. (Malachi 2:2 NASB)

Again, how can our Father's true name be the LORD and His Son's name also be the Lord? In my research, I discovered several reasons why man would unjustifiably want to remove our Maker's true name as noted in an internet article entitled "WHY IS GOD'S NAME MISSING FROM MANY BIBLES?" at: **https://researchsupportsthetruth.wordpress.com/2013/07/08/why-is-gods-name-missing-from-many-bibles/**:

1. anti-Semitic feelings
2. support of trinitarian doctrine
3. money
4. man-made "tradition"
5. superstition
6. "Jehovah" is not the Hebrew way to say God's name.
7. God doesn't need a name.

And at biblehub.com, an excellent online resource for Bible study, you can learn more about how YHVH, which is a transliteration of the original name יהוה, was replaced with substitutions of God and LORD at this page: **https://biblehub.com/hebrew/3068.htm**[8]

Now look at the above quoted verse in the ISR translation below that has restored the original Hebrew name with its Hebrew lettering (יהוה) to the text:

> If you do not hear, and if you do not take it to heart, to give esteem to My Name, said יהוה of hosts, I shall send a curse upon you, and I shall curse your blessings. And indeed, I have cursed them, because you do not take it to heart. (Malachi 2:2 ISR)

---

8 Strong's Concordance, Hebrew: 3068. (Yhvh) the proper name of the God of Israel – **https://biblehub.com/hebrew/3068.htm**

Do you think He is jealous for His name and for His renown? And look at the same verse in the next translation. It helps to look at the same verse in different translations and notice the different ways each translation uses the same word.

> "If you don't listen, and if you don't take it to heart to honor My name," says Yahweh of Hosts, "I will send a curse among you and I will curse your blessings. In fact, I have already begun to curse them because you are not taking it to heart." (Malachi 2:2 Holman Christian Standard Bible)

And in another verse where it is helpful to compare translations, I wondered, "Why was the transliteration "JEHOVAH" (Yahuweh) left in the King James Version in this Psalm but taken out and replaced in the other verses of this same translation?

> That *men* may know that thou, whose name alone *is* JEHOVAH, *art* the most high over all the earth. (Psalm 83:18 KJV)

And most other translations did not retain the transliteration "Jehovah," but changed it to the "LORD" as in the following NASB version:

> So that they will know that You alone, whose name is the LORD, are the Most High over all the earth. (Psalm 83:18 NASB)

How hard would it have been for the King James translators, as well as all the other versions' translators, to just keep the original Hebrew proper name יהוה in the text? My grandson was able to recognize the Hebrew symbols and pronounce them correctly, knowing that they spelled the Father's Name, when he was only seven years old.

And let them know that You, Whose Name is יהוה

, You alone are the Most High over all the earth. (Psalm 83:18 ISR)

It is also interesting to look at Psalm 68:4 in different translations concerning His name.

I found that one definition of "Baal" in Hebrew is the word "lord." This is one of the reasons why I no longer refer to my Heavenly Father or His Son as "the Lord or LORD." The following verse may or may not be literal, but it sure makes you think.

> How long shall there be lies in the heart of the prophets who prophesy lies, and who prophesy the deceit of their own heart, who think to make my people forget my name by their dreams that they tell one another, even as their fathers forgot my name for Baal? (Jeremiah 23:26-27 ESV)

Here is a website I found as I was finishing up this book and saw how important it is to include it here: **The True Set Apart Name of the Creator is יהוה or YHWH (YaHuWaH) in English constants — Warriors Of The Ruwach**

Now look at the following verse in Exodus. I had never thought until recently that this may be describing our Messiah and not an angel.

> See, I am sending a Messenger before you to guard you in the way and to bring you into the place which I have prepared. Be on guard before Him, and obey His voice. Do not rebel against Him, for He is not going to pardon your transgression, for My Name is in Him. (Exodus 23:20-21 ISR)

This messenger has the power to forgive sins, which is an ability only ascribed to the Father and His Son and not to a typical "angel" or "messenger." Did you also notice the last phrase of this verse: "for My Name is *in* Him"? I take this to mean several things, all at the same time: (1) symbolically "name" also means "renown," so this means the Father's renown or reputation is *in* His Son; (2) literally, the Father's name "Yah" is *in* His Son's name "Yahushua."

יהוה is pronounced with the beginning sound "Yah" for "Yahuweh." And יהושע is pronounced with the beginning sound "Yah" for "Yahushua." I like what the ISR has explained in the beginning pages of their translation concerning the "Restoration of the Name" in this verse:

> And Elohim said further to Mosheh, "Thus you are to say to the children of Yisra'el, יהוה Elohim of your fathers, the Elohim of Abraham, the Elohim of Yitshaq, and the Elohim of Ya'aqob, has sent me to you. This is my Name forever, and this is My remembrance to all generations." (Exodus 3:15 ISR)

The ISR[9] explains:

> The reference in this passage is to the Name which, in Hebrew, consists of four letters Yod, Hey, Waw, Hey, and which is frequently referred to as 'The Tetragrammaton.' These letters are often brought across into English characters by the use of the four letters, YHWH (or YHVH). This has been variously pronounced as YaHWeH, YaHoWeH, YaHuWeH, YaHVeH, etc. We have chosen not to enter the pronunciation debate, but rather give the Name exactly as it appears in the unpointed Hebrew text, i.e. יהוה .

And they further state their determination to use the original Hebrew symbols in their translation as follows:

> Secondly, any one of the various attempts to pronounce the Name is infinitely superior to the

---

9   *The Scriptures* published by the Institute for Scripture Research (2009)

actual removal of the Name, and its substitution by an altogether different term! Substitution by a 'good' term does not alter the fact that it is a substitution, a replacement word....

This is what I believe as well. Some believers who are now seeking to pronounce our Father and His Son's Names to the best of their ability use closely pronounced words and spelling to the Names I have chosen to use of "Yahuweh" and "Yahushua." I know that the exact pronunciation may very well have been lost, but this fact still gives us no excuse to substitute other words and titles for their set-apart Names.

Remember my asking if you think that our Heavenly Father is jealous for His name? Look at the following verse from the Old Testament prophet Isaiah:

> I have sworn by Myself; the word has gone out from My mouth in righteousness and will not turn back, that to Me every knee will bow, every tongue will swear *allegiance*. (Isaiah 45:23 NASB)

And you can find this same verse where Paul quotes it in the New Testament:

> For it has been written, "As I live, says יהוה, every knee shall bow to Me, and every tongue shall confess to Elohim." (Romans 14:11 ISR)

Now look at another New Testament verse describing His Son and how Paul states that everyone will bow their knee to Him:

> Elohim, therefore, has highly exalted Him and given Him the Name which is above every name, that at the Name of יהושע every knee should bow, of those in heaven, and of those on earth, and of those under the earth, and every tongue should confess that יהושע

Messiah is Master, to the esteem of Elohim the Father. (Philippians 2:9-11 ISR)

So to whom will everyone ultimately and finally bow down to, the Father or the Son? After studying the above verses closely, what I am reading and understanding is that to our Maker, our Heavenly Father, is who we will be giving esteem to through bowing our knee to His Son and confessing that His Son is Master. Our Heavenly Father shows us that in giving honor and esteem to His Son, we are giving honor and esteem to Him. Yet this fact must not confuse us into believing that in giving them both esteem in this manner, we fall into the lie that they are the same in person. As you read further, I will explain.

Here are some insights concerning our Messiah's name that I discovered.by comparing eighteen translations of this one verse (John 17:11) and getting two very different outcomes between them.

In these twelve translations—NIV, NLT, ESV, Berean Study Bible, Berean Literal Bible, NASB, Christian Standard Bible, Contemporary English Version, Good News Translation, Holman Christian Standard Bible, International Standard Version, and the ISR—all of them have a similar phrase in which the Son refers to the *name* His Father had given Him. He specifically asked His Father to keep them by the power of His Father's name, by saying: "the name that You gave Me."

In the next six translations—KJV, Jubilee Bible 2000, King James 2000 Bible, American King James Version, Webster's Bible Translation, and Young's Literal Translation—their rendering of John 17:11 gives *no mention of the name* that the Father gave His Son, but instead replaces the subject of what or whom the Father gave as being that of the disciples, not a name that was given.

These two phrases from the same verse are completely different in meaning! One has the subject of what His Father gave

Him as "the name," while the other translations have the subject of what His Father gave Him as *those whom* You gave Me," meaning the disciples.

Why make such a big deal about this?

One set of translators clearly shows the Father giving the Son His name, while the other set does not! Isn't it a common practice, even today, for a parent to give part or all of their name to their child? You can see the Father's name "Yah" in His Son's name if their true names are Yahuweh and Yahushua. Can you see the Father's name in His Son's name by using the words God, Lord, Jesus, or Christ as names? I cannot.

Also notice the ending sounds "ah" or "yah" in these words: Hallelujah, Elijah, Isaiah, Jonah, Micah, Zechariah, Jeremiah, and Hannah. In the little Pentecostal church that we attended, the word "Hallelujah" was an often-shouted praise. I heard the meaning of this word was "Praise be to God." The shortened "Yah" fits perfectly now in saying "praise be to Yah" as the correct interpretation of "Hallelujah."

I have found there are many depths to our Father's Word, even as spoken by His Son. Look at what Yahushua says about this in the following verse:

> I have come in my Father's Name and you do not
> receive Me, if another comes in his own name, him
> you would receive. (John 5:43 ISR)

I believe His Son is saying He not only comes in His Father's Name (literally), but He also comes symbolically in His Father's name, which means in His Father's renown, reputation, esteem, and power. Strong's G3686 is the Greek word *onoma,* meaning name, character, fame, reputation, authority, and is translated as "name" in English.

I truly believe when the 1611 translators of the King James Bible took out the true names of the Father and His Son, our enemy had good reason for them to skew, hide, and hinder this knowledge.

Wikipedia says concerning the King James Version:

> King James gave the translators instructions intended to ensure that the new version would conform to the **ecclesiology** and reflect the **episcopal** structure of the Church of England and its belief in an **ordained** clergy. The translation was done by forty-seven scholars, all of whom were members of the Church of England. In common with most other translations of the period, the **New Testament** was translated from **Greek,** the **Old Testament** from **Hebrew** and **Aramaic,** and the **Apocrypha** from Greek and **Latin**. In the **Book of Common Prayer** (1662), the text of the *Authorized Version* replaced the text of the Great *Bible* for epistle and gospel readings (but not for the psalter, which substantially retained Coverdale's Great Bible version) and as such was authorized by Act of Parliament.

Did you notice especially in the very first sentence above, that King James, in instructing his translators, wanted to make sure the Word of our Father would *conform* to the ecclesiology and reflect the episcopal structure of the Church of England instead of the other way around in having the Church of England's doctrine conforming to the Word of our Creator? This was a pretty bold move, don't you think?

Moving on, John 14:28 records the Son saying, "...for My Father is greater than I." They are not the same in person. Can you imagine the confusion of using the words "LORD" for the Father, and "Lord" for the Son, with the only difference being that one is in all caps and the other only has the L capitalized in many translations?

Speaking the same word "Lord or LORD" when we talk can

really promote confusion, too. When my friends say, "The Lord told me" or "Praise the Lord," I can't tell if they mean the Father or the Son. I truly believe it is important to give our Creator and our Messiah their individual and rightful respect. And this is exactly what our Messiah did for His Father.

He clearly had much to say about how He was not the same person as His Father!

> You have heard me say to you, "I am going away, and I will come to you." If you loved me, you would have rejoiced, because I am going to the Father, for the Father is greater than I. (John 14:28 ESV)

> יהושע said to her, "Do not hold on to Me, for I have not yet ascended to My Father. But go to My brothers and say to them, 'I am ascending to My Father and your Father, and to My Elohim and your Elohim.' " (John 20:17 ISR)

His Son, our Messiah, even called His Father "My Elohim." How can they be the same if the following are true?

1. One is greater than the other.
2. The Father sent His Son.
3. One is the Elohim of the other.

This belief that our Father, His Son, and the Spirit are three "godheads in one" is the doctrine of the Trinity that I will have to discuss in another book, as alone it is a very in-depth and complicated research with much information to decipher both factual and false. But I will say that using our Messiah's statement below does not work in justifying a trinity between the Father, Son, and Set-apart Spirit when you compare it to His words in the next two quotes.

> I and the Father are one. (John 10:30 ESV)

And I am no longer in the world, but they are in the
world, and I am coming to you. Holy Father, keep
them in your name, which you have given me, that
they may be one, even as we are one. (John 17:11
ESV)

I do not ask for these only, but also for those who will
believe in me through their word, that they may all be
one, just as you, Father, are in me, and I in you, that
they also may be in us, so that the world may believe
that you have sent me. The glory that you have given
me I have given to them, that they may be one even
as we are one. (John 17:21-22 ESV)

In each and every one of these verses the word "one" is the
Greek Strong's #1520 *heis*. And specifically, in these instances
the word "one" is translated from the Greek *hen* which means *to
be united most closely (in will, in spirit)*. You will see this definition when you click on the following webpage, scroll down to
the Thayer's Greek Lexicon heading, and then under *1b* click on
the highlighted blue references of John 10:30; John 17:11, 21-
23. Doing this takes you to another page where each word of
the verse is broken down and categorized according to its Greek
meaning as well as its original Greek spelling. Here is where
you will see the word *hen*. Visit this link to explore for yourself:
https://biblehub.com/greek/1520.htm[10]

Logically, even without knowing the original Greek meaning
of the word "one" in these references, you can deduct that our
Messiah would never ask the Father to make the disciples on the
same level/godhead as the Father. Our Father, uniquely supreme,
is One and only one, even though He expects us to be "one",
meaning *unified as one*, and set-apart in righteousness with Him

---

10   Strong's   Concordance,   Greek: 1520.   εἷς   (*heis*)   one   –
https://biblehub.com/greek/1520.htm

as His Son is. This is key to understanding our intended relationship with our Maker, His Son, and with each other.

If I were the enemy, I would certainly attempt to bring about confusion concerning the Father and Son's person, purpose, and their names! I can see how it would make it easier in the end times for the anti-messiah to spread his delusions and confusion in denying the Father and the Son and claiming that he is the Creator.

> Who is the liar, except the one denying that יהושע is the Messiah? This is the anti-messiah, the one denying the Father and the Son. (1 John 2:22 ISR)

> Let no one deceive you in any way, because the falling away is to come first, and the man of lawlessness is to be revealed, the son of destruction, who opposes and exalts himself above all that is called Elohim or that is worshipped, so that he sits as Elohim in the Dwelling Place of Elohim, showing himself that he is Elohim. (2 Thessalonians 2:3-4 ISR)

As I learned these facts, it began to make sense that if our Creator and Heavenly Father is so jealous for His name, and He is so detailed, specific, and set-apart, wouldn't He have a unique name, as well as give His Son a unique name?

> She will give birth to a Son; and you shall name Him Jesus, for He will save His people from their sins. (Matthew 1:21 NASB)

This is what we were taught, that the Son of our Heavenly Father is named "Jesus." Yet it is man who gave Him this name after translating it from the Greek Ieousus. This name is Greek. Mary wasn't Greek, and neither was her son. There are no Hebrew words "Ieousus" or "Jesus."

And in the *Strong's Concordance* G2424, "Jesus" is defined as "Iesous": Jesus, the Greek form of Joshua; Jesus, son of

Eliezer; Jesus, surnamed Justus. And Strong's G5547: "Christ" is Christos: Anointed One; Messiah; the Christ.

With all that I've written so far in mind, make note of this fact especially that in my research of the origin of the letter 'J,' I discovered that this letter and its sounding did not even exist at the time of our Messiah. The letter "J" did not come into use in any language until a little over 400 years ago. So Mary, nor any followers or other peoples who lived during those times, could not have called Him Jesus!

In C. J. Koster's book *Come Out of Her, My People*, the word "Christ" or "Christos" is closely related to the pagan Osiris, who was worshipped as "Chrestos." Koster states that Chrestos was a common Greek proper name meaning "good." There's plenty of research out there as to why it is a mistake to associate this name of "Christ" or "Christos" with our Messiah. I won't repeat the work that others have done in proving the connection of the names of other deities with our common and popular usage of the "names" Jesus, Christ, Lord, and God, but you can research this on the net too.

I was saved under the name of "Jesus," and I know that I have had a relationship with Him all my life. I did not know what I know now, and I do believe He honors our humble efforts in doing the best we can at the time with what knowledge we have. Yet it is also up to each one of us to keep on searching for truth and be teachable, humbly praying and discerning what our own actions, obedience, and speech should be as we mature and as our knowledge increases, especially in addressing and talking to and about our relationship with our Maker and His Son. Throughout the Scriptures it is evident that both our Father and His Son take their names seriously.

Personally, Kevin, Mom, and I have now decided to refrain from using the words "Lord, Jesus, Christ, and God" for identifying either the Father or His Son. To the best of our understanding, we are now calling our Messiah "*Yah*ushua," because of all that we have learned and can now see His Father's name "Yah" (from *Yah*uweh) in His Son's name *Yahushua*. To me this is beautiful!

This is also why we have switched to the ISR translation (Institute for Scripture Research) as they have returned the Almighty's name to the text where He had originally placed it in at least 6,823 places.

The ISR includes many other names, such as Mosheh for Moses, Yisra'el for Israel, Sha'ul for Paul, Mitzrayim for Egypt, and so on. Although not perfect, this translation is much closer to helping us understand the true meaning and nature of the inspired words of our Heavenly Father. And another very helpful feature of this translation is found throughout the New Testament of the ISR in that every quote of the Old Testament is written in bold print in the text of the New Testament. Just skimming through this version from Matthew through Revelation, it's amazing to see how full the New Testament is with the words of Law and the Prophets as well as the Psalms from the Old Testament!

C. J. Koster gives further research, noting numerous historical sources concerning not only the words we have wrongly inherited, but also the pagan symbols we mistakenly associate with our worship. And Mr. Koster is another witness for the origin of the word "God" being associated with the German "Gott," which was used as a surname for the deity Odin. He also gives quotes from the *Encyclopedia Britannica*, 11th edition, and *Webster's Twentieth Century Dictionary, Unabridged*, 1st edition, as well as other sources that connect the word "God" to the deities of Teutonic heathen worship.

Our Heavenly Father tells us:

> Now concerning everything which I have said to you, be careful; and do not mention the name of

other gods, nor let *them* be heard from your mouth. (Exodus 23:13 NASB)

Therefore, if there is more than one witness (and I have found many) as to the origin of the word "God" or any other name that I have been using all my life, then I strongly believe I must now be willing to change my behavior in accordance with His commands, once I have learned the truth.

I know for a fact that my Heavenly Father is jealous for His name and does not like any words or behaviors that are used to worship other deities (paganism) to be used or even remotely attributed to Him. You, the reader, can easily research for yourself where these names came from and how our understanding became so clouded.

You will notice I often repeat myself throughout the writing of this book. At first, I was going to correct this occurrence, but upon further thought and in consultation with my mother, who has helped me edit my writings from the beginning, we decided to leave the repetitions of thought and verse in various places in this book. She reminded me of how many times the writers of the Scriptures repeated the Father's and Son's words, as well as their own, to "drive home" a point and the following point is critical in viewing our relationship with our Maker from *His* perspective:

> Do not do so to יהוה your Elohim, for every abomination which יהוה hates they have done to their mighty ones, for they even burn their sons and daughters in the fire to their mighty ones. (Deuteronomy 12:31 ISR)

We are not to use any of the traditions or practices that were used to worship foreign gods (pagan deities)! And we are especially not to say that *their* ways are *for* Him like Aaron did when he used the golden calf to announce a festival *to* Yahuweh (Exodus 32:5). Aaron declared that the children of Israel were going to use that golden calf as a festival/feast to worship Yahuweh. It seems to be human nature to think that it is okay to worship our Heavenly Father in the ways *we want*, even if it means using familiar pagan symbols and traditions to do so, rather than worshipping Him the way he has instructed.

In my research, the historical practice called the "ineffable name doctrine" caught my attention concerning pagan worshipers who had converted to Christianity. They had the belief that it was wrong to invoke the name of their mighty ones, whether it was one of their many pagan deities or the one true Creator. This superstition also influenced the Jewish community with the tradition of not speaking Yahuweh's name but replacing His Name by speaking the words "Adonai" or "HaShem." This belief and practice, called "the ineffable name doctrine," relies on a pagan superstition that Yahweh's name is too sacred to speak. This practice is against His Word, as Scripture tells us to call upon His name as well as to not bring His name to naught (in Exodus 20:7 and Deuteronomy 5:11). "Naught" or "in vain" is Strong's H7723 (shav), meaning "evil, idolatry, uselessness—to nothing." All the following references were helpful to me in researching the topic of calling on Yahuweh's name: 1 Chronicles 16:8, Psalm 105:1, Psalm 79:6, Zephaniah 3:9, Lamentations 3:55, and 1 Kings 18:24.

There must be a very clear separation between our Father's ways and those who serve Him, from the ways of the prince of this world, and those who serve *him*. And I am very certain this includes a clear distinction between our Heavenly Father's name, His Son's name, and the names that are used to identify other deities.

Our thinking was and continues to be that if there is a doubt concerning the traditions and the ways in which we have always loved our Heavenly Father and His Son, then it is worth investigating.

We *cannot* change what was once pagan (unrighteous) into something pleasing, set-apart, and righteous to our Father no matter what our reasoning is for using that behavior, tradition, or practice. We cannot change something pagan into "holy" or "good" by saying, "but that's not what it means to me" or "but this is the way *I* worship my Heavenly Father and Savior."

Once we know our Heavenly Father's true name and His Son's true name, as well as know what the Scriptures reveal concerning their declarations of the importance of their names, how can we deny learning to use them? Even long time Christian artists such as Ron Kenoly are waking up to using the Father's true name in their songs and in his albums: "Set Apart is Your Name Yahuwah volume 1 and volume 2". This is a link to one of his songs declaring the Father's name: **https://youtu.be/R8T-87C0cd6Q** Newer artists like James Block and Hadarah BatYah are also coming on the scene as they use His Set-apart name.

How important is it for us to return to His Word's original language and meaning? In looking around at the moral environment we live in, with its nosedive into prideful perversion, I believe those who see this are also being called to a deeper understanding and knowledge of who our Maker is and of how He really wants us to walk closer to Him—to be set apart—for our good and for our protection in the days to come. This world is much closer, now, to the end of the age than when Paul, Peter, and our Messiah warned us to watch and be prepared!

I ask myself these questions a lot:

- What would the enemy have to gain by making us believe in the names God, Jesus, Christ, and Lord?

- When the anti-messiah comes, what name will he use for himself?

- And will the name he uses be so widely accepted that most will be fooled?

- If you have found out that the true name of your Heavenly Father is not "God" and His Son's name is not "Jesus," how important is it?

CHAPTER 4

*What if you found out our Messiah came to
bring division, even among family members?*

D IVISION? FAMILY IS IMPORTANT! HE gives our
families to us for love and support. Our Maker's design sets up the family system where the woman is
given to the man to be his helper. And the man is the leader, the
provider, and the covering for his wife and his children. Children
are to honor their parents. This is our Creator's Law. If the words
spoken by our Messiah in Matthew 10 are taken literally, that
He came to bring division and not peace, I again thought, *this
doesn't sound right. How can I wrap my mind and heart around
this one?*

Yahushua said the following as He was quoting from the Old
Testament prophet Micah:

> Do not think that I have come to bring peace on
> earth. I did not come to bring peace but a sword, for I
> have come to bring division, a man against his father,
> a daughter against her mother, and a daughter-in-law
> against her mother-in-law, and a man's enemies are
> those of his own household. (Matthew 10: 34-36
> ISR)
>
> For son is despising father, daughter rises up against

her mother, daughter-in-law against her mother-in-law; the enemies of a man are the men of his own house. (Micah 7:6 ISR)

Why would Yahushua, the loving Messiah, who says to uphold the command to honor our father and our mother, make such a statement? Could this be true, that the laying down of our lives for His sake and letting go of the traditions we loved and had always enjoyed with our families as well as in our church homes really cause such division in families?

Sadly, we found it to be true. Again, this is not what we were taught.

At the very same time that we were beginning to distance ourselves from the traditions of Christmas and even Easter, we were also experiencing the division our Messiah was talking about. Some of the most difficult responses to our decisions to love our Heavenly Father with all our hearts by trying to obey His Word came from family. They could not hear that we were *not* trying to accuse or condemn them by our own actions of obedience. It didn't even help for us to try explaining to our loved ones that what we were discovering and becoming convinced of was being revealed to us and maybe just not to them at this time. We simply knew we had to be obedient to what was being revealed to us even though we were not the best at explaining that fact.

Something else we hadn't realized was written by the apostle Paul to Timothy.

And indeed, all those wishing to live reverently in Messiah יהושע shall be persecuted. (2 Timothy 3:12 ISR)

It sure felt like this was what was happening to us, that we were being persecuted. Yet we did not give up! We continued to keep in front of us our most important goal—to love our Heavenly Father with all our heart, soul, mind, and strength by laying down our lives and following the commands being revealed to us.

As a result of our obedience, we were isolated for a time from most of our daughters and their families. Trying to explain ourselves by showing them what we were seeing in the Scriptures, in the beginning, did more harm than good. We finally had to agree to disagree and wait on our Father's timing for healing. It wasn't easy to say "no" to the things they wanted us to continue to participate in during the holidays and also during the weekly Sabbaths. But we knew as much as we loved our families, we could not place pleasing them above pleasing our Heavenly Father and obeying His Word. He had to be first in our lives. We had to trust Him even when we didn't understand why it seemed we were being shunned.

It was difficult for our friends and family too. They tried to figure out what was going on with us by trying to fit us into religious groups and denominations from Mormonism and Jehovah's Witnesses to Judaism, and even saying we were members of a cult. We knew we didn't fit into any of these religious categories. It was so difficult because it seemed we had lost the respect and love of our family, and we could see how difficult and frustrating this was for them too. I'm sure they felt they had lost our love and respect as well. It would have been easier to just give up on honoring the Sabbath in order to honor our family, yet we knew deep down inside what was being revealed to us really was the will of our Father no matter how hard it seemed at the time or how much loss we had to endure.

Who did we love more? We kept on trying to live this truth:

> He who loves father or mother more than Me is not worthy of Me, and he who loves son or daughter more than Me is not worthy of Me. (Matthew 10:37 ISR)

Who were we willing to disappoint or anger more, our family or our Creator? And as we obeyed, trying our best to live what our Heavenly Father and His Son commanded, we kept on praying that our family and friends would be given eyes to see, ears to hear, and a heart to know the truths that we were being shown. To this day, we continue this prayer and refuse to give up on them. For with Yahuweh, all things are possible. He is able to do exceedingly, abundantly, above all that we ask or think, according to His power that works in us.

In the beginning, we really didn't realize just how truly this journey of obedience and coming out of the ways of this world was going to set us apart! Our advice to you, dear reader, is to be diligent in sticking close to His Word, approaching it with a fearful, humble, obedient heart that is led by the Set-apart Spirit of Truth, because there are many spirits masquerading as the real one, enlightening many false teachers. Watch that you do not become the seeds in Matthew 13 that sprang up quickly (discovered the truth) but then withered and died (truth stolen as they were deceived) because of having no root. Also know that our Heavenly Father demands humility as He demanded with King Nebuchadnezzar in Daniel chapter 4. It is an amazing story of pride and humility.

The Creator of the heavens and the Earth and all that is in them demands that His creation worship Him the way He says to worship Him, and to worship Him *only,* no matter what the cost! I truly believe this is "laying down our lives" as His Son modeled and commanded.

In His timing, our family slowly began to communicate with us again. And there has been much healing. To date, they continue to celebrate the popular traditions and do not guard the Sabbath, but they have begun to respect us for our beliefs and have, in fact, found out that we follow no man, cult, or organized religious denomination or group. We believe our family knows we love them, and we will continue to help them in any way we can. We know they love us too and have been there for us, as Kevin and I have been the caregivers for both our moms and have needed and deeply appreciated their help during these critical times.

If you are going through any of these similar circumstances, please be patient, kind, and long-suffering with your friends and especially your family. Don't give in to temptations to retaliate toward those who don't understand, even if they lash out at you in their hurt and anger. All the while, we urge you to stay true and obedient to the truths of His Word that He is revealing, even if you have to endure hardship. Remember, in this world we will have tribulations, but be of good cheer, for Yahushua says, "I have overcome the world." With Yahuweh, all things are possible (Matthew 19:26). There is nothing impossible for our Heavenly Father (Luke 1:37). In the face of much opposition, I believe you will find unspeakable joy and peace even in the middle of a storm. We did! We urge you to be patient and live the following verse:

> And a servant of the Master should not quarrel but be gentle towards all, able to teach, patient when wronged, in meekness instructing those who are in opposition. (2 Timothy 2:24-25a ISR)

It's a narrow road, often hard-pressed, which is what being an overcomer is all about, and it is the best witness to those we love. Sadly, we hear that patience and long-suffering did not prevail for some, as we have seen and heard of husbands and wives separating because one or the other didn't see what was being revealed concerning His commands.

So, our journey continued. We were realizing how much of His Word we had always skimmed over, taking the explanations and interpretations of others as gospel, and never really analyzing or understanding the Scriptures for ourselves. This realization made us read and question more than we had ever done in our lives. Kevin, Mom, and I were beginning to test everything and to learn not to settle for another person's interpretation of our Heavenly Father's Word, no matter who they were. Be careful of falling into the trap of believing what tickles the ears, what is smooth and sounds good to the flesh and easy to follow. I like this saying that I made up when I was writing a note to my granddaughter. It's about truth and lies and a simple way to know the difference.

"Truth is hard to swallow, but lies are easy to follow."

If we like what tickles the ears, what is easy to the flesh, then we end up taking the easy, wide road, and we will miss out on all that He plans on blessing us with. Much of what our Heavenly Father requires goes completely against our carnal thinking and our fleshly desires. His ways are not our ways, and His thoughts are not our thoughts in origin or in the ability to see the entire range of all His plans. His ways and His thoughts are higher than mortal man's.

So even in finding out that following your Savior may very well cause division among family, will you still follow Him no matter what?

CHAPTER 5
*What if you found out our Messiah
did not die on Good Friday?*

O UR *MESSIAH DIED ON GOOD Friday and rose again
on the third day, Sunday*, is what we were taught. But
when you think about it, how do you get three days
and three nights out of him dying on a Friday and then rising
before dawn on Sunday? That is only two nights and two days.

> But He answering, said to them, "A wicked and
> adulterous generation seeks after a sign, and no sign
> shall be given to it except the sign of the prophet
> Yonah. For as Yonah was three days and three nights
> in the stomach of the great fish, so shall the Son of
> Adam be three days and three nights in the heart of
> the earth. (Matthew 12:39-40 ISR)

Remember, truth has layers and layers that build upon more
truth. But lies have layers that build upon each other too. The
father of lies is an imitator of the Father of Truth. So, as we
began to walk out our obedience in removing the pagan celebrations from our lives, as well as learning how our Maker wants
us to guard His Sabbaths and to know His name and His Son's
name, we also began to realize we had believed yet another lie.
There is no way our Messiah could have died and been buried

on a Friday and then risen two days later on Sunday morning. You may think, "What difference does this make?" As you read this chapter you will see that much of the world and the faith community base their actions and practices on this belief alone. Here's the questions I began to ask:

- Where did the belief of a Friday burial come from?

- Who are the religious groups that believe and promote this idea today?

- Is this belief widespread and popular?

- Where in His Word does our Creator tell us to celebrate Easter and give us guidelines for doing so?

- Was the word "Easter" in the original text or did it get substituted in for a different word?

- Was this holiday yet another example of ancient pagan practices and symbolism that have crept into and mixed with our worship and our societies?

- Could it be that by celebrating Easter, we are unknowingly honoring the very same gods and goddesses the pagan Canaanites honored?

- Do witches use some of the same symbols and traditions, like crosses, eggs, bunnies, and decorating trees, especially during the winter solstice at Christmastime, in their pagan worship as Christians do?

As we began to discover the places in which we had been deceived yet again, it wasn't easy. We were ashamed, angry, and shocked at how far-removed from pleasing our Heavenly Father and His Son we had become, all the while thinking that we were loving and honoring them with "our traditions." We found that we were coming to Him and saying the very words spoken through the prophet Jeremiah in Chapter 16:19-21. We have inherited lies!

We didn't want the encyclopedias and historical records to be correct about the connections between ancient pagan worship and today's practice of dying eggs, using images of bunnies, etc. I had fond memories as a child of hunting for that Easter basket of goodies each year that my parents had hidden in the house! And Kevin and I had carried on this tradition for our girls when they were young. Tradition is often familiar and comforting, making it easy to adopt and pass on, especially to our children. We cling to our traditions and don't readily question their origin, whether these actions of ours please our Maker and whether they conflict with our walk as followers of our Messiah. It always boils down to loving and obeying them in this life as we determine our destiny for the next.

So we studied and began to obey each step of truth that we were being shown. And as we did this the fog and confusion slowly began to lift concerning how our Savior's death, burial, and resurrection are intimately connected with the Passover and the Feast of Unleavened Bread, and not with the holiday of Easter! I remember researching on the internet to find out what others (if there were others) were saying about which day Yahushua actually died, and if it wasn't on a Friday. Some websites said He died on a Wednesday, and others said He died on a Thursday. I remember thinking how foreign both of these sounded.

Matthew 12:40 records Yahushua referring back to the Old Testament where Jonah was in the belly of the fish. Why does He make this statement about being in the tomb for three days and three nights? I had grown up celebrating His death on Good Friday and His resurrection two days later.

So, where's the lie?

Could the Easter tradition be yet another one of Satan's mirror images, his imitation of a true and commanded celebration that occurs about the same time?

Could the appointed time of Passover and the subsequent

celebration of the Feast of Unleavened Bread be what we were supposed to commemorate all along?

Is it just a "Jewish thing," or is it an everlasting command for all of His people?

At first, I couldn't wrap my mind around my Messiah dying on any other day than what I had been taught. The only thing I knew for sure was that you can't get three days and three nights out of a Friday afternoon to a Sunday morning. So I continued reading the gospel accounts in Matthew, Mark, Luke, and John about His death, burial, and resurrection, over and over again. I also asked questions from the small Sabbath group we had been meeting with and read some of the teachings and articles on this subject on the internet. I was shocked at how many people seemed to be waking up to the same discoveries we were waking up to!

The Gospel accounts of the Passover when our Messiah, the sinless Lamb, was slain are found in Matthew chapters 26-28, Mark chapters 14-16, Luke chapters 22-24, and John chapters 13-20.

Again, after careful study, and always comparing what others were doing and saying with the Scriptures, I realized that during the week when our Messiah died, there was not only a weekly seventh-day Sabbath but there was also another Sabbath. Some call this Sabbath a "high Sabbath," but it is really another one of our Father's appointed times found in Leviticus 23 as well as in other Scriptures. This other Sabbath was the first day of the Feast of Unleavened Bread (Festival of Matzot), which began on the fifteenth day of Nisan, after the sun went down the evening of Passover, which occurred on the fourteenth day of Nisan. Nisan was the first month of the Biblical new year. It was named Nisan since the time of the Babylonian exile. Remember, our Creator's days begin at sundown the day before and continue to sundown the next day. He does not start at midnight and go to the next day at midnight. To reiterate, a day in Yahuweh's timing is sundown to sundown. Look closely at Genesis 1:5,8,13,19,23, and 31.

Yahushua, our Passover Lamb, was slain between the evenings on the fourteenth day of Nisan. Then He was placed in the tomb before sundown on this same day. To know when this fourteenth day occurred, they counted fourteen days from the new moon or the beginning of the month. And on this fourteenth day there is always a full moon. This is how our Creator set up His timing of months, days, and years. I give more details on this in chapter fifteen of this book. So, taking this information into account, I began to realize that our Messiah's first evening in the tomb began the first night countdown of the three days and three nights that Yahushua gave as a sign (Matthew 12:39-40 and Luke 11:29-30).

And in John 11:9, Yahushua explained a day as containing twelve hours. So if a day has twelve hours and a night has twelve hours, and He said He would be in the grave three days (three twelve-hour periods) and three nights (three more twelve-hour periods), and He was already gone by Sunday morning, then His death would have been on Passover on Wednesday afternoon, then being placed in the tomb before sundown that Wednesday night. This would be the first night, then Thursday night is the second night, and Friday night, the third night. He would not have stayed in the tomb into a fourth night on Saturday night.

Now let's look at each daytime period. The first day in the tomb would be Thursday day, then Friday day, and Saturday day. Three days and three nights He was in the tomb, beginning with Wednesday night. Therefore, He had to have arisen before Sunday morning. And that is why He was already gone by the time the women got to the tomb. Here is a website that will give additional insight into especially the verse of John 11:9 where Yahushua talked about twelve hours in a day: **www.logosapostolic.or/bible_study/RP208-2ThreeDaysNight.htm**

I had always assumed that the gospel accounts depicted Ya-hushua rising on Sunday morning as the sun was rising. This is what I had been taught. Yet, when you understand that the first day of the week began at sundown on the previous night, you realize that He arose just after sundown on Saturday with Mary Magdalene and her companions coming to the tomb very quickly after this as the day was beginning to dawn (start) into the next day, which was Sunday, the first day of the week.

I was never taught to question the traditions we grew up with or to look so intently into the wording and meaning of the Scriptures. Yet now seems to be the time that we all need to take a closer look.

Our inherited traditions of Good Friday, Easter Sunday, and a Sunday morning sunrise service are widely popular and accepted within the faith community as well as in the secular world with all the Easter decorations, candy, and other items of celebration. Banks and government buildings close to commemorate Good Friday. Even the media recognizes these holidays and includes them in their news and weather broadcasts. In contrast, our Father's ways of celebrating and commemorating are not going to be popular or promoted in the world. To honor Him, we have learned that His celebrations should never include the ways pagans used to celebrate their "gods." Knowledge has increased and it is easy to research what is pagan and what is not at the touch of our fingertips. Consider this article about the origins of the sunrise service at **http://wordofyahuweh.weebly.com/easter-sunrise-service.html**

In a later chapter concerning His appointed times, I will explain how we learned to tell when the Passover occurs each year, as well as other feast days according to our Father's appointed times that are not on man's calendar. Knowing when the Passover occurs each year is very important because the month of Nisan in which the Passover occurs is the beginning of our Father's new year that some call the Biblical new year. And knowing this sets the months (new moons) for being able to determine the remainder of His appointed times for the rest of the year.

Kevin and I have had some of the sweetest and kindest Christian friends, who still remain as friends throughout this journey of ours, ask why we no longer celebrate Easter and Christmas. We gently and respectfully give them the history of these practices, share the Scriptures that show our Father's appointed times, and tell them, "It matters how our Father perceives and defines our actions." The common reply has been, "But that's not what these celebrations mean to me."

I know it is hard for all of us to humbly separate from our own perspectives in order to seek our Heavenly Father's perspective that we so desperately need to do in this day and time. We are not angry at these friends, nor they at us. And we still talk and pray for each other to this day!

So again I ask, and desire to challenge you with this question: "What if you found out that the Messiah did not die on Good Friday?" Would you begin to search and see what your Savior would have you believe and then celebrate His way?

CHAPTER 6

What if you found out you can go and sin no more?

D O YOU KNOW THE STORY in John chapter 8 of the woman caught committing adultery? Start reading at verse 1 and read through verse 11, which says in the ISR translation that Yahushua said to her, "Neither do I condemn you. Go and sin no more."

It was *after* meeting the Messiah that the woman was commanded to go and sin no more. Do you think she believed adultery was a sin before she met her Savior? I know that's quite a question to ask. Obviously, she knew she was being accused by the scribes and Pharisees. The reason I ask this question is because there are two main types of sin that can be committed as described throughout the Scriptures. One is described as sinning by *mistake,* as in Leviticus chapters 4 and 5 as well as Numbers chapter 11. Our Heavenly Father knows we make mistakes and sin *unintentionally.* The other type of sinning is deliberate and done intentionally, which is *not a sin by mistake.*

Either way, sin is sin—humankind's actions against the commands of its Creator—intentional or not. We are creations that can be held responsible and accountable for our actions, unlike the living beings (animals) that were also created but not given a conscience to be able to discern what sin and consequences are. It's true that it is in our nature to sin, inherited from Adam and

Eve. It is the curse we were all born under that separates us from a Set-apart and righteous Creator who wants the return of that original clean, pure, complete communion and companionship with man.

Yet Praise the Father that He made a way for us to return to Him. And it is as it was with the woman caught in adultery that only *after* we meet the Messiah do we have the power to go and sin no more as we walk in newness of life, no longer serving sin and its master (see Romans 6:4-7).

This is a good place to discuss our misconception of the command for us to be "perfect" found in Matthew 5:48. We commonly believe that no one can be perfect, everybody sins, and even Christians make mistakes. Yet these facts are never to be an excuse for deliberately sinning. If we do not know the words of our Creator, it is all too easy to fall into the deceit of excusing our sinful behaviors as "normal," "natural," and even "good."

Now look at the following verses and ask, "What is really being instructed here?"

> Therefore you shall be perfect, just as your Father in heaven is perfect. (Matthew 5:48 NKJV)

> Having, then, these promises, beloved, let us cleanse ourselves from all defilement of the flesh and spirit, perfecting set-apartness in the fear of Elohim. (2 Corinthians 7:1 ISR)

> Instead, as the One who called you is set-apart, so you also should become set-apart in all behavior. (1 Peter 1:15 ISR)

> Him, whom we preach; and we teach and we educate every person in all wisdom, to confirm every person as perfected in Yeshua the Messiah. (Colossians 1:28 Aramaic Bible in Plain English)

These are but a few verses calling us to the purposeful action of righteousness (right living/to go and sin no more) according to our Heavenly Father's plan for mankind so that He and we can return to that intended complete relationship of walking and talking with Him as it was in the beginning in the garden.

With just a little research into the original meaning of the word "perfect" found in Matthew 5:48, I learned that it comes from the Greek "*teleios.*" And Strong's G5046 defines it as "(a) complete in all its parts, (b) full grown, of full age, (c) specially of the completeness of Christian character."

We are to grow up in "completeness"—a purposeful and deliberate walk that has the focus of becoming more and more like our Messiah in love and in righteousness. We only have this one life to choose this humble obedience to our Father's commands. As a work in progress, we keep moving toward His command to be set-apart because He is set-apart. We work out our salvation with fear and trembling and do not excuse and confuse our own behaviors as being His will.

Choosing to stay in His commands, to obey the instructions of an all-knowing and all-wise, all-powerful Creator *is* choosing to go and sin no more. Believe it or not, His commands are freedom, freedom from the sin that places us in bondage. This is definitely the opposite of what the world tells us.

> I walk in freedom, for I have devoted myself to your commandments. (Psalm 119:45 NLT)

And His commands are not heavy. They are "do-able."

> For this is the love for Elohim, that we guard His commands, and His commands are not heavy, because everyone having been born of Elohim overcomes the world. (1 John 5:3-4 ISR)

Our Messiah says:

If you love Me, you shall guard My commands.
(John 14:15 ISR)

If we love our Creator and His Son, we will keep their commands. Look at it this way: They love us enough to give us their commands.

> But if we walk in the Light as He is in the Light, we have communion with each other, and the blood of Yeshua his Son purges us from all of our sins. (1 John 1:7 Aramaic Bible in Plain English)

We become new creations without sin through our Messiah's blood that *purges us from all of our sins.* Then through His Set-apart Spirit, we continue to overcome future sin. Isn't this what we are called to do and what we will be rewarded for? If we know His truth, stand firm on it, then His truth will keep us free from the lies of sin and the bondage of the enemy of all mankind? Fools listen to the master of lies, hating instruction from the Creator of life. They believe in the falsehood of thinking and acting as if their own ways are good. They see no evil coming until it is too late.

Look intently at the entire chapter of Jeremiah 23 as well as 2 Timothy chapter 3 with their prophecies and warnings of times to come. Which type of person will you be? What kingdom are you choosing to give your allegiance to and be a citizen of?

Personally, I have resolved to study and stay in the truth, to follow its wisdom and humbly trust it, and to empty myself of my own stubborn ways that go against my Maker's design. From the beginning, this is how man was to live and love Him and others.

If we know the truth, searching for it with the fear of Yahuweh as if searching for precious gold, then we are truly free to expect and receive the good He has for us.

Fear יהוה , you His Set-apart ones, for there is no

lack to them who fear Him! Young lions have lacked and been hungry; But those who seek יהוה lack not any good *matter*. (Psalm 34:9-10 ISR)

Otherwise, we are fools if we think any other way is freedom, blessed, peaceful, rich, or without dire consequence. His paths of righteousness do not change. If we want to be free and stay free, we will follow His Commandments, holding them close in our hearts so that we do not sin against Him.

I have hidden your word in my heart that I might not sin against you. (Psalm 119:11 NIV)

We *can* go and sin no more.

CHAPTER 7
What if you found out the Law was never abolished?

A LMOST EVERY CHRISTIAN DENOMINATION TEACH-ES the Law was abolished when our Messiah died for our sins. Yet He says He did not come to abolish it:

> Do not think that I have come to abolish the Law or the Prophets; I have not come to abolish them but to fulfill them. (Matthew 5:17 NIV)

Study just this verse a minute and notice several things. First, He made His statement twice. "Do not think that I have come to abolish...." And then again in a different way, He says, "I have not come to abolish...." He sounds pretty firm in wanting there to be no mistake or misinterpretation here.

Second, He states "Law and Prophets" *together*, that He has not abolished. Have you ever heard anyone teach that the Prophets have been abolished? I haven't, and I've listened to a lot of teachers and preachers over the years.

Third, the way our Messiah says, "I have not come to abolish them but to fulfill them," shows that "to fulfill" is contrary to "to abolish." He did not come to abolish *but* instead to fulfill. You can see these two words, *abolish* and *fulfill,* must have opposite meanings. Fulfill cannot mean the same as abolish just in looking at how they were stated. And we haven't even looked at their Greek definitions yet.

Fulfill is *"pleero"* in Greek and means to make full, to complete. The word 'fulfill' means to universally and absolutely fulfill, so in the context of Matthew 5:17, it means to cause God's will, as made known in the Law, to be obeyed as it should be, and God's promises, given through the prophets, to receive fulfillment.

Why would Thayer's Greek Lexicon say such a thing in making the Law sound like it should be obeyed instead of abolished?[11]

Abolish in Greek, according to the Thayer's Greek Lexicon Strong's NT #2647, is *kataluó*, which means "to deprive of force, annul, abrogate, discard.[12]"

So you see, "to render full" or "to complete" does not at all mean to deprive of force, annul, abrogate, or to discard. When our Messiah completed His mission on Earth of living a sinless life so He could offer himself as a sacrifice for the sins of the world, He did not annul, abrogate, or discard His Father's Law, but completed it and brought it into full view!

You may also be thinking of this verse:

> For Christ is the end of the law for righteousness to everyone who believes. (Romans 10:4 NASB)

The word "end" does not mean abolish. It is from the Greek word *"telos,"* meaning "aim, goal, outcome, purpose, fulfillment." The Law points to our Messiah like a telescope aims your focus at a particular view. He is the aim or goal of the Law. In the next few pages you will see the connection between the Law and our Messiah even clearer.

---

11   Thayer's Greek Lexicon: 4137. πληρόω (*pléroó*) to make full, to complete – **https://biblehub.com/thayers/4137.htm**

12   Thayer's Greek Lexicon: 2647. καταλύω (*kataluó*) to deprive of force, annul, abrogate, discard – **https://biblehub.com/thayers/2647.htm**

But what do the words "the Law" mean? I began to think of what I had grown up hearing about "the Law," and in my Christian upbringing, which was mainly Southern Baptist, I don't remember much teaching about it other than statements like "The Law was a system of sacrifices the original Israelites performed, and Jesus died on the cross and took it away because He was the last sacrifice."

So, I realized I had always equated "the Law" with the Old Testament system of sacrifices. I had also learned the categories or divisions of the books of Scripture and that the first five books (Genesis, Exodus, Leviticus, Numbers, and Deuteronomy) were a division called the books of Law, but that's about as far as my understanding of the Law went after all those years in church. Now, from reading through the five books of the Law each year according to a reading cycle, I have learned so much and how interesting the true and historical stories of the relationships our Creator started with mankind from Adam to Noah, Abraham, Isaac, Jacob, Joseph, Moses, and so many more. These books are filled not only with our Father's commands but with promises and commitments, curses and blessings. When you read these accounts, especially with the understanding that they directly relate to us, you will find, as we did, a closer and more understanding bond with your Maker and His Son. Here is a link that gives an example of several different ways that the books of Scripture are put in divisions:

**https://biblehub.com/library/gerberding/
the_way_of_salvation_in_the_lutheran_church/
chapter_v_the_divisions_of.htm**

And speaking of divisions, I want to briefly introduce the fact of there being quite a few people who believe the Law itself is divided into three categories: moral, civil, and ceremonial. This perspective sounded good to me at first. Yet the more I studied the commandments of the Law, the more I realized our Heavenly Father never placed them in categories the way man is trying to do.

While memorizing and teaching the Ten Commandments during our "church years," it never occurred to me that even these commandments were actually contained *within* the Law that I was being told went away when my Savior came and died. This would have been a good point to make when we were first beginning to keep the Sabbath, food laws, and Feast Days and were told by others that in doing so, we were being legalistic. Now I know if this were the case, then trying to obey the laws of the Ten Commandments had to be legalistic too, since they are contained within *the Law*. Our Messiah, Yahushua, even stated that *all* the Law and the Prophets *hang* on the two commands to love Yahuweh with all our heart, soul, and mind and to love our neighbor as ourself. See Matthew 22:36-40 in your copy of His Word.

Most Christian denominations focus on the New Testament books from Matthew to Revelation for obeying the commandments. Yet where do you think each and every one of the commandments in the New Testament came from? They *all* came from the Law and the Prophets contained in the books of the Old Testament.

I know I said to read Matthew 22:36-40 in your own translation, but this next revelation is too important to miss so I'm going to quote these verses from the ISR in order to use the Father's and Son's names. Notice that the ISR translation uses the Hebrew transliteration *Torah* for the word *Law*. Throughout this book you will see me using the word Torah for Law interchangeably.

Really pay attention and contemplate the last sentence in this quote:

> Teacher, which is the great command in the Torah?
> And יהושע said to him, "You shall love יהוה your

Elohim with all your heart, and with all your being, and with all your mind." This is the first and great command. And the second is like it, "You shall love your neighbour as yourself." On these two commands hang all the Torah and the Prophets. (Matthew 22:36-40 ISR)

Also look at this more common translation of that last verse:

On these two commandments hang all the law and the prophets. (Matthew 22:40 KJV)

This word "hang" in Greek is Strong's G2910 meaning to "hang" or "suspend from," and only occurs in the entire New Testament in this one verse. To hang does not mean to sever or stop from being attached. The Law and the Prophets *hang onto* these two greatest commandments—they "hang" together.

We *cannot* live out the completion of these two commandments without the detailed instructions of the Law and the Prophets. So when we are told these two great commandments our Messiah quoted in the above verse replace the Law and the Prophets and that obeying these are all that we need, it is another grave misinterpretation of Scripture. These two great commandments are the summation of details listed in the Law and Prophets, and without them, how are we supposed to exactly love our Heavenly Father with all our heart and love our neighbor as ourself?

And these two great commandments are also written *within* the Law, right along with all the other commands in the books of Law. Look at Deuteronomy 6:5 and Leviticus 19:18, and you will find these two commandments. Didn't the above question to Yahushua by one of the Pharisees in Matthew 22:36 say, "which is the great command *in the Torah*?" Yahushua's answer never stated or even alluded to any of the commandments in the Law being replaced by these two greatest commandments.

When Our Heavenly Father gave the Law to the ancient Israelites, He expected them to learn His commands *right where they were*, even though they could not complete many of them in the context of the wilderness in which they were living at the time. This was true especially with the commands pertaining to land ownership, how to sow their seeds, harvesting, and even when to let their land rest. There was no land ownership while they were still wandering in the wilderness on their journey to the promised land. Yet they were expected to learn His Law containing all these commands and to keep the ones they could obey while wandering in the wilderness. These included relationships, what is defined as food for human consumption, the Sabbath, the Ten Commandments, and many more. This is no less true of us today. We are still alive, heaven and earth are still here, and we are wandering in the wilderness, so to speak, waiting to get into the promised land, and there are commands that we cannot complete either. But it doesn't mean they "went away."

I will continue, throughout this book, to give you more details concerning the commands we can and cannot keep because of the time and place in which we are living. And prayerfully I can answer some of the questions I'm sure you're beginning to have. I still have questions too. I don't have all the answers even though I have found many as I keep on searching. And I do know that as long as we live, we are to search for our Creator and what pleases Him. Our Heavenly Father is not an ambiguous Creator. He spells things out in detail and reveals His secrets in His timing. This does not release us from the following verse I memorized as a young child:

> Do your utmost to present yourself approved to Elohim, a worker who does not need to be ashamed, rightly handling the Word of Truth. (2 Timothy 2:15 ISR)

Now I want to discuss another misinterpretation that leads us astray. When the words "the Law" and even just the word "law" are being used, especially in the writings of Paul, they can be in reference to a single law/principle or can be in reference to a group of laws, or even to the entire body of the Law, which is also referred to as the Mosaic Law. It's like using the words "law of physics" to sometimes refer to a single and specific law, and at other times referring to the entire body of the "law of physics."

To assume the entire body of the Law is being referred to, particularly in verses that discuss *not being under law* or *being dead to the law*, is a grave error!

As I am writing these pages, I happened to catch an advertisement on YouTube that played just before my worship music. It was a discussion of whether the Law was relevant and should be obeyed in this day and time. As I listened, they quoted the following statement of Paul as their reasoning for teaching that we are no longer obligated to obey the Law today:

> For sin shall not be master over you, for you are not under the Law but under grace. (Romans 6:14 NASB)

This widely quoted verse of Romans 6:14 is used by many preachers and teachers as one of the main examples for saying we are not responsible to obey the commandments of the Law. This is false doctrine! As you read the next few paragraphs below, you will begin to see what I mean.

Now look at Paul's other statements that seem to completely contradict the above verse *if* he really was talking about the entire body of *the Law* with its commands in Romans 6:14:

> Do we then nullify the Law through faith? Far from it! On the contrary, we establish the Law. (Romans 3:31 NASB).

> So then, the Law is holy, and the commandment is holy and righteous and good....For we know that the

Law is spiritual; but I am fleshly, sold into bondage to sin. (Romans 7:12,14 NASB)

Now I'm going to use the ISR translation in the following verses. And remember, *torah* means law:

For I delight in the Torah of Elohim according to the inward man. (Romans 7:22 ISR)

Here is yet another verse that really shows you whether Paul is talking about a single law/torah or the whole body of commandments of the Law:

For the torah of the Spirit of the life in Messiah יהושע has set me free from the torah of sin and of death. (Romans 8:2 ISR)

Clearly two different laws are being referred to, the first being the *torah of the Spirit* that sets us free, and the second being the *torah of sin and of death* that our Maker created from the beginning that demands death for man's transgressing against His Law. Our Messiah did not set us free so that we can then do what we want regarding His Father's commands. Yet this is exactly what we are taught!

And look at Paul's letter to the Galatians where he is describing the same thing but in different words:

Messiah redeemed us from the curse of the Torah, having become a curse for us—for it has been written, "Cursed is everyone who hangs upon a tree." (Galatians 3:13 ISR)

Can you see how understanding these two verses is key to understanding the seemingly controversial and confusing verses Paul wrote in the New Testament?

Romans 6:14, 8:2, and Galatians 3:13 are all talking about the same thing! Paul is not talking about the entire body of the Law in these instances. He is talking about the curse of the specific law of sin and death! We have all sinned (Romans 3:23) and fall short, condemned, and desperately in need of redemption!

So when you look at these three verses together you can easily see that no longer being under the *curse of the Torah* is a good thing to be set free from. We are no longer under this law's condemnation. Halleluyah!

And when you look at Paul's other statements above about the Torah being established by faith, you know he is not talking about something that was taken away. The Torah is a body of commandments that is holy, righteous, good, and spiritual that Paul says he delights in. It makes no sense to say the Law is good on one hand and then say it is abolished and no longer to be obeyed on the other hand.

Our mindset of thinking the Law has been abolished is exactly the lie our enemy wants us to swallow and one of the many angles he uses to deceive us so that we sin against our Creator by ignoring His commands we *can* keep.

If we read the next verses below, of this commonly misunderstood chapter in Romans, with the knowledge that we now have, we will clearly see why Paul can call the Law/Torah good and spiritual, yet say he has died to the Torah (its curse that demands death):

> So my brothers, you also were put to death to the Torah through the body of Messiah, for you to become another's, the One who was raised from the dead, that we should bear fruit to Elohim. For when we were in the flesh, the passions of sins, through the Torah, were working in our members to bear fruit to death. But now we have been released from the Torah, having died to what we were held by, so that we should serve in newness of Spirit and not in oldness of letter. What, then, shall we say? Is the Torah sin? Let it not be! However, I did not know sin except through the Torah. For also the covetousness I knew not if the Torah had not said, "You shall not

covet." But sin, having taken the occasion through the command, did work in me all *sorts* of covetousness. For apart from Torah sin is dead. And I was alive apart from the Torah once, but when the command came, the sin revived, and I died. And the command which was to result in life, this I found to result in death. For sin, having taken the occasion through the command, deceived me, and through it killed *me*. So that the Torah truly is set-apart, and the command set-apart, and righteous, and good. Therefore, has that which is good become death to me? Let it not be! But the sin, that sin might be manifest, was working death in me through what is good, so that sin through the command might become an exceedingly great Sinner. For we know that the Torah is Spiritual, but I am fleshly, sold under sin. (Romans 7:4-14 ISR)

Through our Messiah's death, we too die to the torah/law of sin and death. It cannot hold us. We were dead in our trespasses because we are flesh and sold into bondage to sin. The only way to satisfy what this specific law demands (its curse), is for death to occur. We are to die for our sins. But our Creator, in His great love and planning, provided a substitute to take our place. The only one who could break that curse was His only begotten Son in the form of a sinless human being. *Now we are no longer under law but under grace.* He didn't even take away that law either—He satisfied its demand. Grace means favor. Our Heavenly Father through His Son did us a favor and paid our penalty! He *did not* take away the need for us to follow His instructions for living as He outlined in His commands in the body of the Law. We will bear fruit to Him through the Spirit if we have truly believed and repented (turned) from our sins.

Our Messiah's resurrected life occurred when the Spirit of Yahuweh raised Him from the dead, thus defeating the *curse* of the Law. And without His resurrection we have nothing! This was the final act in defeating that curse. When our sinless Messiah died, He did not stay dead! And the *torah/law of the Spirit of the life in Messiah* in the above verse is talking about the law/principle of the Spirit that sets us free from the bondage of sin when we place our faith in the Son, Yahushua. You see there are many meanings and uses of the word "law."

I can't say this enough! We have to be careful not to immediately assume, every time we see the words *the law*, that what is being discussed is the entire body of our Father's commands that make up the Law/Torah.

Look at this very misunderstood statement Paul made about the Spirit and the law:

> But if you are led by the Spirit, you are not under the law. (Galatians 5:18 NKJV)

We are no longer under the Law's condemnation *if* we are led by the Spirit.

Remember the list of the fruit of the Spirit ending in this statement: *Against such there is no law* (Galatians 5:23b). When we walk in the Spirit, we produce the fruit of the Spirit: "love, joy, peace, patience, kindness, goodness, faithfulness, gentleness, and self-control. Against such there is no law." There is no law against these actions because they are from the Spirit, which is always in compliance with the Law. Therefore, when we are led by the Spirit, we cannot be condemned or judged by the Law. This is what *no longer under the law* means. Remember this verse?

> There is, then, now no condemnation to those who are in Messiah יהושע, who do not walk according to the flesh, but according to the Spirit. (Romans 8:1 ISR)

We receive the Spirit of Truth only when we repent and accept the Messiah as our Savior.

Now Paul makes sense when he says the Torah/Law is spiritual and righteous and good. When we walk in the Spirit, which leads us in compliance with the Torah, we do not invoke the penalty of the law of sin and death. You sin, you die is the most basic way to describe this penalty. It's not an immediate death, but *knowingly* and *defiantly* (Hebrews 10:26) walking in sin will eventually lead to the worst kind of death, which is a forever separation from our Creator and a forever torment with our enemy in the lake of fire (Revelation 20:12-21:8 and Revelation 14:11).

Now, I'm going to quote just a few verses in Romans 8 beginning with verse 1 again and continuing through several verses that clearly show the Spirit is connected to the Law/Torah as it helps us fight against our fleshly sin. Through the Spirit we have the desire and the power to overcome our flesh. We are told to not quench the Spirit! Please take the time to read these two chapters together and carefully: Galatians chapter 5 and Romans chapter 8, remembering what you have learned in the above paragraphs.

And note that the below verses also show the different uses and meanings of the word "torah/law" as it discusses both the torah of the Spirit and the torah of sin and death as well as the Torah of Elohim (the entire body of the Law, also called the Mosaic Law):

There is, then, now no condemnation to those who are in Messiah יהושע, who do not walk according to the flesh, but according to the Spirit. For the torah of the Spirit of the life in Messiah יהושע has set me free from the torah of sin and of death. For the Torah being powerless, in that it was weak through the flesh, Elohim, having sent His own Son in the likeness of flesh of sin, and concerning sin, condemned sin in the flesh, so that the righteousness of the Torah should be completed in us who do not walk according to the flesh but according to the Spirit. For those who live according to the flesh set their minds on the *matters* of the flesh, but those *who live* according to the Spirit, the *matters* of the Spirit. For the mind of the flesh is death, but the mind of the Spirit is life and peace. Because the mind of the flesh is enmity towards Elohim, for it does not subject itself to the Torah of Elohim, neither indeed is it able, and those who are in the flesh are unable to please Elohim. (Romans 8:1-8 ISR)

What are we set free from?

We are set free from the torah/law of sin and of death, *not* from obedience to our Father's commands in the Law!

The righteousness of the Torah is completed in us as we walk according to the Spirit's leading in righteousness. Righteousness starts with our repentance and belief in Yahushua for the forgiveness of our past sins, but it is not complete until we walk (and continue to walk) in that righteousness according to the Spirit, which never goes against the Law. This is being perfect, which means to be complete as our Messiah commanded in the following verse.

Therefore be perfect, as your Father in the heavens is perfect. (Matthew 5:48 ISR)

Subjecting ourselves to the Torah of Elohim is how we are able to please our Heavenly Father and to be like Him in righteousness. We don't have to second-guess Him. We know through the Torah what He wants from us and how to stay in His will.

In looking at just these few statements of Paul's alone, and there are many more in his letters, especially when you take the time to read through the entirety of the chapters in Romans, how can we believe Paul is telling the Romans or the Galatians or anyone else *not* to obey the Law? This is like saying do not obey righteousness. Paul even says the Law defines what sin is in Romans 7:7, as well as in the following verses:

> And we know that whatever the Torah says, it says to those who are in the Torah, so that every mouth might be stopped and all the world come under judgment before Elohim. Therefore by works of Torah no flesh shall be declared right before Him, for by the Torah is the knowledge of sin. (Romans 3:19-20 ISR)

Look at this same verse of Romans 3:20 in the NASB version:

> Because by the works of the Law none of mankind will be justified in His sight; for through the Law *comes* knowledge of sin. (Romans 3:20 NASB)

How is all the world able to come under judgment if the Law does not address the whole world's sin? It's not just a "Jewish thing" as many would have us believe. The work of the Law (its job) is to define sin, teach everyone what sin is, and then our Creator uses it to judge the world's sin. It's also a rod and a sword and a guideline that not only defines sin, but also defines righteousness, thus separating sinful actions from righteous actions. The Law points us to our Messiah for what He has done and what He will do in the future as it outlines our Creator's appointed times of Sabbaths including His seven annual Feasts.

Below is another verse that, when taken out of context, is misunderstood and misquoted. The Law/Torah of Mosheh itself cannot declare us right as even the writer of the book of Acts wrote:

> Let it therefore be known to you, brothers, that through this One forgiveness of sins is proclaimed to you, and by Him everyone who believes is declared

right from all *sins* from which you were not able
to be declared right by the Torah of Mosheh. (Acts
13:38-39 ISR)

The Law was weak through the flesh (Romans 8:3). We have
all sinned and fall short (Romans 3:23). Therefore, by works,
whether *our* working or *Its* working of bringing us the knowledge of sin—we cannot be justified by it. The judgment of the
Law shut us all up under sin (Romans 3:9, 22; 11:32) until it
was time (Galatians 3:22-23). Then the Savior we needed came
in *apart from* the Law, which means *to the side of, without the
intervention of or cooperation of the Law.*[13]

Now look at these next two verses that use the words *apart
from* and *without* that mean the same thing:

But now, apart from the Torah, a righteousness of
Elohim has been revealed, being witnessed by the
Torah and the Prophets. (Romans 3:21 ISR)

For we reckon that a man is declared right by belief
without works of Torah. (Romans 3:28 ISR)

And look at the same verse as above in the NASB translation, as it is very helpful to compare the same verses in several
different translations, especially KJV, New King James, ESV,
NASB, NIV, and NLT. You can also compare different translations online, using websites that give multiple versions on a
single page and include tools for research of Greek and Hebrew
meanings. The website I use most often is biblehub.com.

For we maintain that a person is justified by faith
apart from works of the Law. (Romans 3:28 NASB)

The Torah is not "of" belief. It didn't originate or "come
from" belief. It is "to the side of" (apart from) belief. The Torah

13   Thayer's Greek Lexicon: 5565. χωρίς (*chóris*) separately, apart –
https://biblehub.com/greek/5565.htm

was written down and given to Moses and points us toward the Savior. Then, without (apart from) the Torah came belief, in and through our Messiah justifying us, which then in turn established the Torah (see Romans 3:31). We've got to get things in the right order!

Where justification (salvation) from our transgressing the Torah "comes in" is *before* we do any "good works" of the Torah. We cannot be justified by our works or we never would have needed a Savior! Do you now see where our enemy has tripped us up in the order of our understanding of the Father's plan?

Therefore, it makes no sense for Paul to tell us not to subject ourselves to the Torah of Elohim through which the Spirit leads us.

First, through faith and faith alone, then are we obligated to obey the Law. Trying to obey the Law in order to be justified (to be saved) is wrong—it's backward! And I repeat, it negates our need for a Savior. Through the Law comes the knowledge of sin that points us to our need for a Savior. Then through our faith and repentance of turning away from the sin that the Law pointed out to us, we can walk as our Savior walked in the power of the Spirit in righteousness according to the commands in our Heavenly Father's Law.

I repeat. We've got to get things in the right order and untwist what Satan has twisted!

And teaching the Gospel without teaching the Law as John Wesley warns (see my reference to this below) makes us lawless and licenses us to live the way we want because we defined for ourselves what sin is. That was never the plan!

These false teachings take away our instructions and our boundaries, even our knowledge of how to stand and fight against sin. We have to be able to identify sin to fight against it. Remember Paul said he did not know sin except through the Law.

The Torah is a thoughtful, loving boundary put in place by a loving Father as instructions to his children that tells us we can go just so far and still be safe from harm. Here is an excellent illustration my friend Peggy shared with me. One day some educators decided to remove fences that surrounded a school playground, thinking that they needed to open up the boundaries and give the children a greater sense of freedom. But they received entirely different results when the fence was removed. They found the children huddled in the middle of the playground in fear because their boundary lines were gone. The fences had provided a hedge of protection just like our Father provides through His Law of commands. He knows better than we do what we need, what keeps us safe from bondage. And He provided those boundaries for us in His Word. We need only take great care to understand His intended meanings rather than man's alterations and misleading interpretations to truly benefit from His guide book.

Somewhere along the way during all this searching for the truth concerning the Law, I stumbled upon the word "antinomianism." I'd never heard this word before. I was searching for the Greek meanings of "lawlessness" and "law." "Lawlessness" in Greek is Strong's G458 "*anomia.*" And "law" in Greek is Strong's G3551 "*nomos.*" According to the *Merriam-Webster Dictionary*, "antinomianism" is from the medieval Latin "*antinomus,*" which is derived from the Latin "*anti*" and the Greek "*nomos,*" which means "anti-law." So a believer in this concept is called an "antinomian." *Merriam-Webster* has two definitions for an "antinomian," as follows:

> "1) One who holds that under the gospel dispensation of grace, the moral law is of no use or obligation because faith alone is necessary to salvation. 2) One who rejects a socially established morality."

Do you see how our enemy takes a truth,e.g., *faith alone is necessary to salvation* and adds to it a deceitful and generalized twist to wrongly conclude, *therefore the Law is of no use or obligation?*

Take a look at the link to this short paper called "The Minutes of the Conference of 1744":

John Wesley and the Conference of 1744 (imarc.cc)

In this paper, John Wesley discusses his firm campaign against antinomian teachings. He knew that faith and obedience must go together. And as you read, think about where we are today with our church doctrines that have so readily adopted an antinomian (anti-law) approach. Whether directly or indirectly, these doctrines have encouraged society to embrace more and more of the immoral lifestyles of the world, all of which is *against the Law* (antinomianism), because the Law is not taught as necessary for moral living. You need only look at the stance that the pope and the Roman Catholic institution takes in dictating to the masses that their change of the Sabbath to first-day worship and even the embracing of homosexuality and abortion are not against our Creator and His design for mankind.

I don't understand all the commandments, not even in all of the verses; for example, in chapters 18-20 of Leviticus. But the commands that I do understand, while I am learning and studying His Word day in and day out, I cannot ignore. The following verse is in the Law:

> Do not hate your brother in your heart. Reprove you neighbour, for certain, and bear no sin because of him. Do not take vengeance or bear a grudge against the children of your people. And you shall love your neighbour as yourself. I am יהוה. (Leviticus 19:17-18 ISR)

These commands occur right in the middle of this Leviticus chapter that started in verse 2 with the command to be set apart because our Father is set apart. You see, if we were taught that the Law has not been abolished and we actually studied it to see *what commands we can keep* in this day and time, we would know that the above command to forgive and to love our neighbor is in the Law, and then you'd think that it would not be said that the Law has been abolished.

There are more commands in Leviticus 19 regarding the eating of meat with blood, divination, magic, shaving, slandering, not letting our livestock mate with another kind, etc. Yet I can see that all these verses contained within Chapter 19 of Leviticus—all of them are His Laws! Some I understand and can easily obey, and others I am still studying, seeking His Set-apart Spirit to help me rightly divide His word of truth (2 Timothy 2:15) to know how and when to apply them to my life. It takes careful study and discernment to know whether a commandment or instruction is historically a onetime deal for certain people (such as to Moses, Aaron, and the Levitical priesthood for leaving Egypt, crossing the Jordan, fighting battles, ceremonial cleansing, etc.) or whether it's a commandment intended for all mankind for all time from ancient times to the end of times who are willing to be called "His."

> *We make a grave mistake in assuming and teaching*
> *the generality that His Law has been abolished!*

While many of the commands recorded in the books of Law have been reiterated by our Messiah and His apostles, many have not. Yet these commands should not be brushed aside as irrelevant. For example, the following command, as far as I can determine, is not specifically stated in the New Testament and is only found in the body of the Law of the Old Testament:

> And do not have intercourse with any beast, to defile yourself with it. And a woman does not stand before

a beast to mate with it, it is a perversion. Do not defile yourselves with all these, for by all these the nations are defiled, which I am driving out before you. (Leviticus 18:23-24 ISR)

The above two verses are listed right after this one concerning male relations that *is* reiterated in the New Testament several times:

And do not lie with a male as with a woman, it is an abomination. (Leviticus 18:22 ISR)

Preaching and teaching that the Law has been abolished paves the way for all kinds of deceitful reasoning and behaviors, no matter if these laws, or even a resemblance of them, have been reiterated in the New Testament by our Messiah Yahushua and the apostles—or not!

If you believe Yahushua changed His Father's Laws into His own commands, requiring us only to follow what He specifically quoted from the Old Testament, then that would mean bestiality is permissible because the Messiah, in the New Testament, does not specifically command against that behavior. This is ludicrous thinking, isn't it? But that's exactly how many people are splitting hairs in order to do what they want!

And popular Protestant Christian doctrine shies away from obedience to our Father's commands as its doctrine focuses more on love, prosperity, and faith (without works). Don't get me wrong—love, prosperity, and faith are excellent pursuits, but fall very short of the necessity of the fear of our Creator and obeying His commands. Isn't it our "works" that we are going to be judged by, because this is the *proof* of our faith and our love? See Revelation 20:12. I pray you will know the truth concerning faith and obedience in the following verses:

But according to your hardness and your unrepentant heart you are treasuring up for yourself wrath in the day of wrath and revelation of the righteous judgment of Elohim, who "shall render to each one according to his works": everlasting life to those who by persistence in good work seek for esteem, and respect, and incorruptibility; but wrath and displeasure to those who are self-seeking and do not obey the truth, but obey unrighteousness; affliction and distress on every human being working what is evil, of the Yehudi first, and also of the Greek; but esteem, respect, and peace to everyone working what is good, to the Yehudi first and also to the Greek. For there is no partiality with Elohim. For as many as sinned without Torah shall also perish without Torah, and as many as sinned in the Torah shall be judged by the Torah. For not the hearers of the Torah are righteous in the sight of Elohim, but the doers of the Torah shall be declared right. (Romans 2:5-13 ISR)

And to whom did He swear that they would not enter into His rest, but to those who did not obey? So we see that they were unable to enter in because of unbelief. (Hebrews 3:18-19 ISR)

As I was looking especially at the ending words *did not obey* in verse 18, and then compared them to other translations, I noticed the following:

And to whom sware he that they should not enter into his rest, but to them that believed not? (Hebrews 3:18 KJV)

And to whom did He swear that they would not enter His rest, but to those who did not obey? (Hebrews 3:18 NKJV)

Do you see the very different ending between these two

translations? Out of all the translations on Biblehub.com, as well as the ISR translation, only the ISR and the King James versions use the words *unbelief* and *believed not,* respectively. All the rest of the translations used the words *did not obey, disobedient, disobeyed.* Why the difference? I immediately investigated the original wording in the Greek and found that it is Strong's Greek 544 *apeitheo,* which means to disobey. And the Thayer's Greek Lexicon says that this particular verse means to refuse *belief and obedience.* My conclusion is that you cannot separate obedience from belief and some translations picked the subject concerning obedience while others picked the subject of belief/faith as the reason He swore they would not enter into His rest. Either way this is additional proof to me that our belief and our obedience go hand in hand.

If we say we are believers in Yahushua, we already know that faith alone is necessary to *obtain salvation.* But what happens next, after we have repented and turned from our sins? We get all tripped up after that, because we are not taught that to *continue in that salvation,* to work it out with fear and trembling, we must strive to walk in obedience to the Law, which is that newness of life—Yahuweh's original plan for man to live and to love Him and each other. We must keep the commandments!

If we live *lawlessly,* living how we see fit in our own eyes, then we are going against the way we were designed and against our Creator's intentions. Look at this truth proclaimed by the Prophet Jeremiah:

> O יהוה, I know the way of man is not in himself,
> it is not for man who walks to direct his own steps.
> (Jeremiah 10:23 ISR)

We were never meant to come up with our own blueprint. However, we *were* given the ability to choose whether we want to follow our Maker's design or not. Without His guidelines in His Word, especially without the details in His Law, we *will* call evil good and good evil. Isn't this what is happening today? We were warned about lawlessness in so many places in Scripture:

> And because of the increase in lawlessness, the love of many shall become cold. (Matthew 24:12 ISR)

> And then I shall declare to them, "I never knew you, depart from Me, you who work lawlessness!" (Matthew 7:23 ISR)

> The Son of Adam shall send out His messengers, and they shall gather out of His reign all the stumbling-blocks, and those doing lawlessness, and shall throw them into the furnace of fire—there shall be wailing and gnashing of teeth. (Matthew 13:41-42 ISR)

> For the secret of lawlessness is already at work—only until he who now restrains comes out of the midst. (2 Thessalonians 2:7 ISR)

Even when Yahushua spoke of the condition of lawlessness, as he called the Jewish leaders "lawless," He was specifically referring to their lack of keeping His Father's commands in the Law. These Sadducees and Pharisees made up their own man-made laws and standards, which are also called *dogma* and *traditions of men,* that made them lawless and hypocrites. Yahushua scolded them, as seen in the following verses:

> Forsaking the command of Elohim, you hold fast the tradition of men. (Mark 7:8 ISR)

> So, you, too, outwardly indeed appear righteous to men, but inside you are filled with hypocrisy and lawlessness. (Matthew 23:28 ISR)

> And יהושע answering, said to them, 'You go astray, not knowing the Scriptures nor the power of Elohim.' (Matthew 22:29 ISR)

Don't you think this is true of us today? We go astray because we don't know, nor take to heart the commands of our Heavenly Father. The commands in His Law keep us on track and provide a hedge of protection—a boundary that also serves as a filter for the deceits in life that are thrown at us. We must have this knowledge and conviction so we can recognize lies, especially in the latter days when false prophets and false messiahs are leading many astray (Matthew 24).

I tell my grandchildren: "The more truth you know, the less lies you believe."

Satan wants us far from the truth. And he's done a very good job throughout the centuries in making us believe that obeying the Law is somehow "sin" on our part as well as making us believe it is no longer relevant. He has separated our faith from our obedience so we are easily deceived. Faith and obedience go hand in hand just like John Wesley said in the paper referred to above, "The Minutes of the Conference of 1744."

And I truly believe the world, *being led astray,* is what has to come. And then the man of lawlessness is revealed. He has to get us away from the understanding of what righteousness is so we don't recognize it. The world lies. And its deceit has crept into our churches over the centuries as our enemy's way of furthering what Paul predicted in the following verses:

> Let no one deceive you in any way, because the falling away is to come first, and the man of lawlessness is to be revealed, the son of destruction, who opposes and exalts himself above all that is called Elohim or that is worshipped, so that he sits as Elohim in the Dwelling Place of Elohim, showing himself that he is Elohim. (2Thessalonians 2:3-4 ISR)

How else do you think he is going to be able to lead people astray than if they do not know the difference between righteousness and lawlessness?

This falling away from the truth must come before the end of this age. And where better for Satan to deceive us than in our assemblies? Our enemy does not want us walking as our Messiah walked in the commands of His Father.

The apostle John also speaks out against this falsehood:

> Whoever commits sin also commits lawlessness, and sin is lawlessness. (1 John 3:4 NKJV)

So there's your definition of what the Law is not—it is not sin. Preachers and teachers today are telling us not to sin, yet at the same time they are telling us we don't have to obey the Law. What a paradox! No wonder there is so much confusion and falling away from the faith!

Now be very careful with the interpretation of this next verse:

> Because the Law worketh wrath: for where no law is, *there is* no transgression. (Romans 4:15 KJV)

At first glance, this verse sounds like the Law is something we might want to get rid of in our lives that causes transgression. If you do an internet search for "Pastor CD Brooks Law and Grace Made Simple," you will see one of the simplest explanations of the above verse in this YouTube video[14].

Lawlessness is our nature, and we cannot overcome it unless we have *both faith and obedience* in our lives. Faith comes by hearing and hearing by the Word of Yahuweh. And the Word of Yahuweh is the Law as well as the Prophets. Faith is through our Messiah who is the Word made flesh—the full view.

We have to have *both* the witness of the Messiah (faith) and the Word of our Creator (Law) to overcome sin (Revelation 12:11). We can't separate the Word (the Law) from our Messiah. They are inseparable. He obeyed the Law, and we are to follow His example.

I'm reminded of Yahushua's words: "I am the way, the truth,

---

14   **https://www.youtube.com/watch?v=P-QYn7S7qow**

and the life." Look at His connection to the Torah/Law as "the way, the truth, and the life" in Psalm 119:

Way:

> Blessed are the perfect in the way, who walk in the Torah of יהוה. (Psalm 119:1 ISR)

Truth:

> Your righteousness is righteousness forever, and Your Torah is truth. (Psalm 119:142 ISR)

Life:

> If Your Torah had not been my delight, I would Have perished in my affliction. Let me never forget Your orders, For by them You have given me life. (Psalm 119:92-93 ISR)

Our enemy comes at us from so many angles of deceit. And the biggest lie he has is in making us believe that Yahushua came to abolish the Law so we will sin and commit the very trespasses that caused us to need a Savior in the first place. I've said this before, but it was worth repeating.

Another excuse I often hear is: "The Law is not for us; it was for the Jews back in the Old Testament times." I can see where this thinking comes from, as the Law was first written down and given to the original Israelites, often referred to as the Jews. They have been guarding many of the laws to this day in their keeping of the annual Feast Days, the Sabbath, and the food laws. Because of this we are often told that the keeping of these commands are "Jewish" and not for Christians. Why then are we not told the same thing when we try to obey the Ten Command-ments of the Law, well, all but the Sabbath law?

Yet the Law is for all mankind. Think about it, if all men have sinned, and sin is defined by the Law, doesn't it make sense that all men and not just the Jews will be held accountable to live by the Law?

There is even evidence in the Scriptures that our Creator's Law for how He wants mankind to live was revealed at the beginning of His creation long before it was ever written down and given to Moses on Mt. Sinai.[15] Think about it. How did Cain and Abel know what and when to bring offerings to Yahuweh? How did Noah know what clean and unclean animals were? Why does Scripture record that Abraham obeyed Yahuweh's requirements, commands, decrees, and laws long before they were ever given to Moses? (Genesis 26:5)

We have discussed some of what the Law is, what it is not, our need for it, misinterpretations of *who* the Law is for, and even *how* the words "the law" can easily be mistaken in certain verses for the entirety of the body of the Law when it should be understood that a single law or principle within the Law is being discussed. This is especially true when quoting the apostle Paul in several but very critical instances.

Let's look at another one of his easily misunderstood verses in Ephesians 2:15 where we have been taught, as soon as we hear the word "abolished," to immediately equate it with "the Law." I have quoted this verse in two different translations below:

> ...having abolished in His flesh the enmity—the torah of the commands in dogma—so as to create in Himself one renewed man from the two, thus making peace. (Ephesians 2:15 ISR)

> ...having abolished in His flesh the enmity, *that is*, the law of commandments *contained* in ordinances, so as to create in Himself one new man *from* the two, *thus* making peace. (Ephesians 2:15 NKJV)

---

15   **Did Abraham Keep the Same Commandments God Gave to Moses?** | **United Church of God (ucg.org)** https://www.ucg.org/bible-study-tools/booklets/the-new-covenant-does-it-abolish-gods-law/did-abraham-keep-the-same-commandments-god-gave-to-moses

Just as we analyzed Matthew 5:17 at the beginning of this chapter, let's study this verse closely. Note the punctuation and word choices by each translator is slightly different, yet they both define the *enmity* as being what was abolished. The ISR translation connects the abolishment of the enmity with the *torah of the commands in dogma* by a dash (—). In comparison, NKJV connects the abolishment of the enmity with the *law of commandments contained in ordinances* by using the words "that is." At first glance and with no other points of reference in Scripture being thought of, we easily, but mistakenly, assume these connections to mean the Law was abolished by our Messiah and that this law is the Mosaic Law.

Remember this assumption does not match Yahushua's words about the Law in Matthew 5:17 that He did not come to abolish the Law, nor Paul's words in Romans 3:31 and 7:12, 14, and 22 that the Law is established by faith and it is set-apart, righteous, good, and spiritual.

So, having established this fact, by the very words of Yahushua as well as Paul's other statements that indicate the Mosaic Law is relevant and has not been abolished, we then ask, "What *law of commandments contained in ordinances* is Paul really talking about in Ephesians 2:15?" Taking my own advice to study the surrounding verses, let's look at it:

> Therefore remember that you, once nations in the flesh, who are called 'the uncircumcision' by what is called 'the circumcision' made in the flesh by hands, that at that time you were without Messiah, excluded from the citizenship of Yisra'el and strangers from the covenants of promise, having no expectation and without Elohim in the world. But now in Messiah יהושע you who once were far off have been brought near by the blood of the Messiah. For He is our peace, who has made both one, and having broken

down the partition of the barrier, having abolished in His flesh the enmity—the torah of the commands in dogma—so as to create in Himself one renewed man from the two, thus making peace, and to completely restore to favour both of them unto Elohim in one body. (Ephesians 2:11-16 ISR)

What enmity did Yahushua abolish in His flesh? What favor needed to be restored between man and Elohim?

Remember our discussion a few pages back concerning what was against us? It was the law of sin and death. It was a curse that condemned, separated, and placed a barrier between us and our Maker. Refer again to Romans 8:2 and Galatians 3:13. But let's back up to the beginning of the above verses and see if this conclusion plays out.

Paul begins by addressing the gentiles who are also called *nations* or *the uncircumcision.* He tells them they were excluded from the citizenship of Israel, strangers from the covenants of promise that were given to Abraham and his descendants and were without Elohim (Yahuweh). But through the blood of Yahushua, nations/gentiles have been brought into these promises and included in the spiritual citizenship of Israel.

Then Paul states the Messiah is our peace who has made both uncircumcised (nations/Gentiles) and circumcised (Jews) *one,* after breaking down the partition of the barrier which is Strong's 3320: *the middle wall, partition wall, barrier* and Strong's 5418 *a hedge, fence, partition.* In other words "the middle wall of the wall."

I did a search for the words "middle wall of the partition" and discovered an interesting article at **https://www.biblestudytools.com/encyclopedias/isbe/partition-the-middle-wall-of.html**. It gives the history of a wall between the inner and outer court area of the temple in Jerusalem around the time of Paul's writing. This wall was not a tall barrier, but more like a fence that kept the Gentiles from being allowed farther into the Temple where the Jews could go. I do believe Paul used this language of a middle dividing wall as a symbolic example of the Jew and Gentile being separated and then coming together without a "dividing wall" between them. Yahushua leveled the playing field, so to speak, for both Jew and Gentile to become "one." He did this by showing that both have transgressed the Law, both were in need of a Savior, and both became "one renewed man." Therefore, through Yahushua they are no longer in the position of hostility toward Yahuweh through their transgressions, but both Jew and Gentile are now in a position of peace and favor, completely restored unto Elohim in one renewed body.

A second example that can also symbolize Paul's description of a middle wall or partition being broken down by the Messiah is the partition or the veil that was torn in two at the moment Yahushua died (Matthew 27:51, Hebrews 9:3-12). This veil within the walls of the temple that Herod built was quite tall, possibly 60 feet high, and very thick. It was ripped or torn from top to bottom simultaneously with the moment of Yahushua's death. This veil had separated the most Set-apart Place (the Holy of Holies), where the presence of Yahuweh dwelt, from the rest of the Temple where men dwelt.[16] The barrier being broken, through the ripping of the veil, signified man was no longer separated from Yahuweh's presence. And through His Son, our Messiah, we can now go directly into the presence of our Heavenly Father.

Whether either one or both of these physical examples of a barrier or wall that was broken down are what Paul is using to give us a symbolic picture of the peace that now exists between all mankind and our Maker (including both Jew and Gentile), *the fact remains, the enmity was abolished—not the Law.* Yahushua met the requirements of these ordinances (dogma) contained in the Law that were against us, that required death for our trans-

---

16   **https://www.gotquestions.org/temple-veil-torn.html**

gressions and produced enmity (hostility) between men and Elohim. Now through Yahushua's blood sacrifice, He is our peace.

There is another view for explaining the *commands in dogma/the commands contained in ordinances* in the above verse. I do not adhere to it and will briefly explain why. The word "dogma" is also used to describe decrees or ordinances of men such as in Caesar Augustus's decrees (dogma) in Luke 2:1 and Acts 17:7. Then there's the oral torah, also known as the Talmud or traditions of men. In Paul's day, the Talmud was specific to the Jew for their ideas on how to carry out the commands in the Mosaic Law. It had nothing to do with Gentiles being required to adhere to it. So to make these traditions or decrees of men fit as an explanation for the *commands in dogma/the commands contained in ordinances* in Ephesians 2:15, the abolishment of these commands of men would have to have created a renewed man in Elohim and brought peace. I do not see that this scenario fits.

This brings us to Colossians 2:14, where Paul uses the same word, "dogma," for ordinances as he did in the above verse of Ephesians 2:15 as being against us. Because of what we learned in the previous paragraphs, much of this analysis will sound familiar, so let's just dive right in and look at Colossians 2:14 in four different translations:

> Blotting out the handwriting of ordinances that was against us, which was contrary to us, and took it out of the way, nailing it to his cross. (KJV)

> …having blotted out that which was written by hand against us—by the dogmas—which stood against us. And He has taken it out of the way, having nailed it to the stake. (ISR)

> …having canceled the certificate of debt consisting of decrees against us, which was hostile to us; and

He has taken it out of the way, having nailed it to the cross. (NASB)

…having wiped out the handwriting of requirements that was against us, which was contrary to us. And He has taken it out of the way, having nailed it to the cross. (NKJV)

Ordinances/decrees/requirements/dogmas in each of these translations is Strong's Greek 1378 "dogma." And in this verse as well as the previously discussed verse of Ephesians 2:15, Paul uses a specific form of the word dogma called "*dogmasin*" that is only used in these two scripture references. This furthers the evidence that Paul is absolutely talking about the same enmity in both of these cases that was against us and was taken away by our Messiah.

Now let us look at four interpretations of what people think the meaning of Colossians 2:14 is. The most common and accepted interpretation of this verse today is that the Mosaic Law (Law of the Old Testament) was taken away/abolished. However, we have proven this interpretation does not line up with the Scriptures we have just studied.

The second interpretation is less common, but there are some who believe the *certificate* (as noted above in the NASB translation) is the certificate of divorce Yahuweh wrote to adulterous Israel in Jeremiah 3:8. This explanation is unlikely as the certificate of divorce was only written to adulterous Israel in Jeremiah 3:8 and not to both Jew and Gentile, as Paul indicated when he said the certificate was against "us" (meaning both Jew and Gentile as he was also addressing the Gentile believers in Colossae).

A third interpretation we previously discussed is that this "dogma" was the oral torah or Talmud. This interpretation does not fit either, as the Talmud of the Jewish leaders were decrees aimed at the Jews and not the Gentiles. And as I just stated, Paul makes it clear that he is including both Jew and Gentile when he talks about "us" in this verse. It also makes no sense to say the Jews, having written the Talmud themselves, wrote a certificate of debt.

Fourth is the interpretation that many are beginning to understand today. This interpretation of Paul's words, whether translated as *the certificate of debt consisting of decrees* or *the handwriting of ordinances that was against us,* fits the fact that the Law is still established yet the *penalty* of the ordinances/decrees/dogma were judgments within the Law demanding our payment for transgressing against it. This "certificate of debt/handwriting of ordinances" is a debt we, both Jew and Gentile, owed as a result of the law of sin and death. It was definitely taken away by our Messiah when he nailed it to the stake (cross). And it was definitely against us! Knowing what we know to this point, this fourth explanation more than any of the other explanations makes the most sense.

I want to make it very clear that none of the Laws, not even this law of Colossians 2:14, was abolished. Instead, the *condition* it demanded, that was against us, was met! That condition was taken away and abolished, not the Law, as is commonly and traditionally misinterpreted and mistakenly taught.

Another area that is helpful for comparison in which Paul *really is* talking about traditions of men and elementary matters of the world as *dogmas* is also in Colossians chapter 2. As you read these verses, you will also see that here too, Paul's message is commonly misinterpreted:

> Therefore, as you accepted Messiah יהושע the Master, walk in Him, having been rooted and built up in Him, and established in the belief, as you were taught, overflowing in it with thanksgiving. See to it that no one makes a prey of you through philosophy and empty deceit, according to the tradition of men,

according to the elementary matters of the world, and not according to Messiah. (Colossians 2:6-8 ISR)

If, then, you died with Messiah from the elementary matters of the world, why, as though living in the world, do you subject yourselves to dogmas: Do not touch, do not taste, do not handle—which are all to perish with use—according to the commands and teaching of men? These indeed have an appearance of wisdom in self-imposed worship, humiliation and harsh treatment of the body – of no value at all, only for satisfaction of the flesh.(Colossians 2:20-23 ISR)

Let me start with a little background. Paul was writing his letter to the new believers in Colossae, a city in the Mediterranean that was full of pagan practices and philosophies, which included Gnosticism. The city was largely populated by pagan Gentiles as well as a Jewish population. The little assembly at Colossae, which was mainly made up of former pagan Gentiles, was coming out of the ways of the world as new believers in Yahushua. They were learning to keep Yahuweh's festivals, which are also called His feast days, that included celebrations of eating and drinking that the Gnostics did not approve of. Gnosticism included the practice of ascetism, a belief in which one is spiritually elevated through harsh treatment of the body that Paul is calling "of no value at all." These Gnostics had no tolerance for festival eating and drinking. This Gnostic tradition is what Paul was condemning as he would have never condemned the set-apart observances of the Father's festivals, new moons, or Sabbaths, nor would he have called His Father's commands elementary matters of the world.

Paul condemned the *traditions of men*. Sadly, most Christians have been taught to believe just the opposite. We easily overlook the fact that these new believers in Yahushua were being taught to observe the eating and drinking associated with Yahuweh's appointed Feast days, His set-apart times, just as Paul and Ya-hushua observed. This is why Paul specifically listed these things in his instructions to the Colossians, telling them not to let any-one judge them for keeping these laws except for their own body of believers. I'm going to repeat Paul's condemnation in another translation below:

> If you died with Messiah to the elemental forces of this world, why do you live as if you still belonged to the world? Why do you submit to regulations: "Don't handle, don't taste, don't touch"? (Colossians 2: 20-21 Holman Christian Standard Bible)

Let's back up to Colossians 2:8-23 to get a better overview of all these points that we have just discussed:

> See to it that no one makes a prey of you through philosophy and empty deceit, according to the tradition of men, according to the elementary matters of the world, and not according to Messiah. Because in Him dwells all the completeness of Elohim-ness bodily, and you have been made complete in Him, who is the Head of all principality and authority. In Him you were also circumcised with a circumcision not made with hands, in the putting off of the body of the sins of the flesh, by the circumcision of Messiah, having been buried with Him in immersion, in which you also were raised with Him through the belief in the working of Elohim, who raised Him from the dead. And you, being dead in your trespasses and the uncircumcision of your flesh, He has made alive together with Him, having forgiven you all trespasses, having blotted out that which was written by hand against us—by the dogmas—which stood against us. And He has taken it out of the way, having nailed it to the stake. Having stripped the principalities and

the authorities, He made a public display of them, having prevailed over them in it. Let no one therefore judge you in eating or in drinking, or in respect of a festival or a new moon or Sabbaths—which are a shadow of what is to come—but the Body of the Messiah. Let no one deprive you of the prize, one who takes delight in false humility and worship of messengers, taking his stand on what he has not seen, puffed up by his fleshly mind, and not holding fast to the Head, from whom all the Body—nourished and knit together by joints and ligaments—grows with the growth of Elohim. If, then, you died with Messiah from the elementary matters of the world, why, as though living in the world, do you subject yourselves to dogmas: "Do not touch, do not taste, do not handle"—which are all to perish with use—according to the commands and teachings of men? These indeed have an appearance of wisdom in self-imposed worship, humiliation and harsh treatment of the body—of no value at all, *only* for satisfaction of the flesh. (Colossians 2:8-23 ISR)

When you look at all of these verses together, you can see that our Messiah stripped the authority of the law of sin and death by meeting its terms. He did not strip away His Father's Law. Again, it is clear that Paul would never call the Law of Yahuweh "elementary matters of the world" knowing that he calls the Law "good, righteous, spiritual, and being established by faith," and he says he delights in it! Seriously, would Paul then turn around and tell the Colossians to stay away from something that he says he personally delights in? Misinterpretation of the writings of Paul leads to the false teaching that the Law has been abolished, making us think it does not apply to our lives today.

And speaking of traditions and commandments of men,

Yahushua also condemned the Jewish leaders for their false teachings in Matthew 23. He further reinforced the need for His followers to continue to guard and do the teachings of the Law.

> Then יהושע spoke to the crowds and to His taught ones, saying, 'The scribes and Pharisees sit on the seat of Mosheh. Therefore, whatever they say to you to guard, guard and do. But do not do according to their works, for they say, and do not do. For they bind heavy burdens, hard to bear, and lay them on men's shoulders, but with their finger they do not wish to move them.' (Matthew 23:1-4 ISR)

"To sit on the seat of Mosheh" was to teach the Law from that place of authority (both literally and symbolically) like Moses did when he sat teaching and rightly ruling the people from the authority of the commands of the Law.

And look at what Yahushua scolded the scribes and Pharisees for when He quotes the prophet Isaiah as this prophesy was coming true in them:

> You hypocrites! Well did Isaiah prophesy of you, when he said: "This people honors me with their lips, but their heart is far from me; in vain do they worship me, teaching as doctrines the commandments of men. (Matthew 15:7-9 ESV)

From what we have just discussed, you can see that false interpretations and false doctrines started a long time ago. And thinking even further back, the deception of our Creator's words began in the garden. Misinformation just keeps getting passed down from generation to generation.

Our enemy will stop at nothing to twist our Creator's Word, to lure us away from the knowledge of how to love, serve, honor, and worship Yahuweh His way. Deceit and the use of confusion are his specialties, and he does not want us to know what pleases our Creator, what protects us from evil and judgment, nor how to stay within the loving and beautiful will of our Heavenly Father.

So, with all these predispositions, we have mistakenly approached and taught the New Testament writings and especially some of Paul's writings with a bias that causes us not to look for obedience to the Law being connected to our faith. We separated "the Law" of the Old Testament from the "commands" that our Messiah said to keep in Matthew 19:17 when He was asked by the rich young ruler how to inherit eternal life. His response was:

> And he said to him, "Why do you ask me about what is good? There is only one who is good. If you would enter life, keep the commandments." (Matthew 19:17 ESV)

We have studied quite a few verses showing the Law has not been abolished and how obeying it is relevant and necessary in our relationship with our Heavenly Father. Yet you still may have to work through, as I did, some more individual verses where it still looks like Paul is against our obedience to the Law. There is not time in this book to go through every verse that has been misinterpreted in this way. But I pray I have shown you how to take our Creator's Word, really investigate it, compare it to other truths in Scripture and in building upon that knowledge to really understand its meaning. Remember that looking at a single verse to draw a conclusion, especially about something as important as our Father's commands are, we must read more verses and chapters to understand, especially to understand Paul.

Peter warned us in 2 Peter 3:15-16 that Paul is hard to understand in some of his letters. But the more you read his all letters to the assemblies (churches) in the books of Romans, 1 and 2 Corinthians, Galatians, Ephesians, Philippians, Colossian, and 1 and 2 Thessalonians, you will understand that Paul never goes against any other teaching in the Scriptures. Keep treasure hunting. And ask as you study each of Paul's letters: "What are the similarities between them? Does he expound more in some than in others in defining a particular subject or word? When Paul uses the word "law," is he talking about the entire body of commands in the Law or is he talking about a single principle or law within the whole body of the Law?

And as you search, keep a humble, teachable heart, knowing that not everything we have heard or have been taught is scriptural, but much of it is doctrine—man's doctrine, that easily twists and tickles the ears. We must test everything we hear, every interpretation of His Word, by searching His Word *for ourselves.*

I could go on and on in pointing out verses from Psalm 119 as well as from the Prophets and the book of James that promote the goodness and necessity of obeying our Father's commands in His Law.

And Yahushua firmly gives us how long the Law with be relevant in the verse after He declared that He did not come to abolish the Law or the Prophets. I want you to look at this in the following three translations:

> For truly I tell you, until heaven and earth disappear, not the smallest letter, not the least stroke of a pen, will by any means disappear from the Law until everything is accomplished. (Matthew 5:18 NIV)

> For assuredly, I say to you, till heaven and earth pass away, one jot or one tittle will by no means pass from the law till all is fulfilled. (Matthew 5:18 NKJV)

> For truly, I say to you, till the heaven and the earth pass away, one yod or one tittle shall by no means pass from the Torah till all be done. (Matthew 5:18 ISR)

In the end, each of us will be held accountable for our walk that is our works. What did we do with our salvation? Did we become saved to go back into sin? Or are we working out our salvation with fear and trembling and not walking away from it after receiving the Good News? How do we know how to walk like our Messiah walked? What defines sin? How else would we turn away from salvation but by our actions against His Law? These actions will be judged by a measuring rod and by the Word coming from the mouth of our Messiah that divides and is sharper than any two-edge sword.

If all men have sinned, and sin is defined by the Law, doesn't it make sense that all men, both Jew and Gentile, will be held accountable as to whether they lived by the Law or not?

Simply put, the Law tells us what is right, what is wrong, what makes our Creator angry and will bring everlasting punishment on us if we continue to choose our own ways instead of His. It reveals His righteousness that does not change. His Law is His commands.

I pray that by now you know that it *does* matter whether you obey the Law. Your destiny in the next life depends on it. It is time to wake up and get the truth so we can start living the truth, now. The time is coming very soon, I'm afraid, when we will have to make some tough choices. And without the foundational truths of the Word combined with the leading of the Set-apart Spirit of Truth through Yahushua, we will find ourselves deceived and on the wrong side, becoming an enemy of Yahuweh. This is not where I want to be, nor do I want any of my family or friends in this place either.

So I ask, *if you have found out that the Law has not been abolished*, will you let your Heavenly Father shape and form your life through His commandments in the Law, or will you walk away and pay the price later? If you have realized this, and

I pray you do, the Scriptures will begin to reveal many more verses of truth confirming the forever continuance of His Law. Your humble obedience will open up more wisdom and knowledge of who He is and what He is going to do than ever before!

CHAPTER 8
What if you found out you cannot complete
many of the commandments?

W OULD THIS BE A REASON to not search out His commandments that you *can* complete? By now I pray this is not the case and that you believe it really does matter to search for your Maker's heart through His commands in His Law that you can complete.

In a previous chapter, I promised that I would give further details surrounding the commands we cannot complete and why. In the back of the ISR translation is a section called *Explanatory Notes*, where the translators outline the difference between today's governing bodies as opposed to a judicial system set up within the framework of a Torah-based nation. Below is a quote from the ISR translation:

> Law: a. In the Tanak (pre-Messianic Scriptures): (5) Much of the Torah involves commands, laws, right-rulings, statutes, etc., which relate to a properly constituted society, such as that which prevailed under Mosheh or under the sovereigns of Yisra'el. As such, laws which clearly apply within a civil or national context are not to be misapplied by individuals living in a society that is not totally subject to the Torah as

its constitution and legal code. Thus, for example, you may not decide to stone someone to death for violating the sabbath. The decision would have to be made by a judge within the framework of such a Torah-based nation. Clearly then, although these laws are still applicable, since the context in which they are to be applied is lacking at present, they can only be applied when such a Torah-true nation comes into existence (for example, when Messiah returns to set up his Reign).

As we began to research the Law we also found that over half (really, a majority) of the 613 laws in the Torah pertain specifically to actions we cannot complete given the time and society in which we live. These include the following:

- priesthood duties
- going to war and the command to not return to Egypt
- donations to the temple
- Nazarite vows
- instructions for building the altar
- instructions for maintaining the altar and its use
- judicial laws for punishment
- laws for slave ownership
- burnt offering instructions
- grain offering instructions
- drink offering instructions
- land ownership instructions

So mistakenly concluding that the entire body of the Law, with its commandments, is of no regard on the basis that there are many we cannot keep is a grave mistake. This mindset negates our responsibility in completing the very important commands that are still relevant to our lives that provide a hedge of protection from the bondage of sin and that teach us how to walk as our Messiah walked in newness of life.

In the beginning of our walk to obey the Sabbath and while we were learning about Yahuweh's other laws, misunderstanding Christians chided us by saying that in our keeping of the Sabbath or even in following Yahuweh's food commandments, we would have to keep the laws of sacrificing animals as well as keep all the other 600-plus laws in the Torah. At this point we could have become discouraged and given up on following the few commands that we knew our Heavenly Father had just shown us. But we didn't give up. We kept on digging into His Word.

And while we were learning, we knew that in no way would we ever sacrifice animals, not even on Passover! Yahushua atoned for our past sins, but in doing so, He did not take away our future responsibility to not sin against His Father's commands.

> And He Himself is an atoning offering for our sins, and not for ours only but also for all the world. And by this we know that we know Him, if we guard His commands. The one who says, "I know Him," and does not guard His commands, is a liar, and the truth is not in him. But whoever guards His Word, truly the love of Elohim has been perfected in him. By this we know that we are in Him. The one who says he stays in Him ought himself also to walk, even as He walked. (1 John 2:2-6 ISR)

We have got to get back to looking at our Maker's commands in His Law for living from our Savior's perspective and not from ours! Think about how He lived and walked on this earth? Can we not obey the commands in the same manner through the power of the Set-apart Spirit? To deny Its power I do believe is blasphemy against this Spirit.

As we have already discussed, it makes no sense for someone to tell us we should not obey the laws against stealing, adultery, murder, sexual immorality, etc. Yet when it comes to obeying other laws of observing the Sabbath and the annual Feast days, food laws, the wearing of clothing, etc., we are told these were done away with and we are not responsible to obey them. I really don't see any difference in any of these laws other than humans categorizing them according to what is convenient for their flesh and makes sense in their own eyes. As we tried to obey the commands that were being revealed to us and that we could keep, we were even called "extreme" and "legalistic." These assumptions and misinformation definitely tried to discourage us.

Yet, I get it. As humans, we are stubborn and do not like denying our flesh. In our carnal nature, we do not readily search for more things to obey, not even if they are the Words and design of an all-knowing, all-powerful Creator, that detail how to please Him. We like doing things our way, desiring not to give up our self-determination and independence for allegiance to another. We kick against the goads, the very boundaries that protect us and give us our independence from bondage. Our Maker knows our tendencies. He knows and warns in His Word of how we want to direct our own lives rather than being led. It's easy to sit in church and let our preachers and teachers focus more on having faith and not as much on obeying the commands. It's easy to feel that we are "good to go" after taking that first step of repentance and belief. I have a friend that says too many times people feel they have their "fire insurance" once they have asked for forgiveness and accepted the free gift of salvation. They feel that further actions of obedience or even disobedience will have no bearing on their salvation. Yet take a look at the following verses that speak strongly to the contrary:

> So that, my beloved, as you always obeyed—not only in my presence, but now much rather in my

> absence—work out your own deliverance with fear and trembling, for it is Elohim who is working in you both to desire and to work for *His* good pleasure. Do all matters without grumblings and disputings, in order that you be blameless and faultless, children of Elohim without blemish in the midst of a crooked and perverse generation, among whom you shine as lights in the world, holding on to the Word of life, for a boast to me in the day of Messiah, that I have not run in vain or laboured in vain. (Philippians 2:12-16 ISR)

And remember what I shared in Chapter 2 that my Pentecostal pastor taught me about how we can walk away from our salvation?

> For it is impossible for those who were once enlightened, and have tasted the heavenly gift, and have become partakers of the Set-apart Spirit, and have tasted the good Word of Elohim and the powers of the age to come, and fall away, to renew them again to repentance—having impaled for themselves the Son of Elohim again, and put Him to open shame. (Hebrews 6:4-6 ISR)

You see, that *good Word of life* and the *Word of Elohim* are still describing His instructions on how to live—His Law. And salvation is that "tasting" of the Good News of forgiveness that cancels the penalty for our *past sins*. We accepted His gift from heaven when we first believed and repented. But there is more. This gift came with a complete and total cleansing of sin the Law could not erase. However, it does not at all mean His Law on how to live righteously has been erased. Once enlightened, as it says above, we are not to turn back or fall away from right living. Walking in this newness of life means leaving sin behind, learning to walk even as our Messiah walked, to overcome sin through the power of the Set-apart Spirit. And this is outlined in detail in the Law and the Prophets that He quoted and lived by. He gives a full view of His Father's commands.

> If we confess our sins, He is trustworthy and righteous to forgive us the sins and cleanse us from all unrighteousness. (1 John 1:9 ISR)

> ...who gave himself for us to redeem us from all lawlessness and to purify himself a people for his own possession who are zealous for good works. (Titus 2:14 ESV)

Sure we are going to stumble and make mistakes, but we are not to pridefully and defiantly stay there. We are not to fall away and walk in a life of our own leading, which is sin. As discussed earlier, we have no right to redefine what sin is.

This next verse is very scary for me to even think about, especially when it comes to the ones I love. I fear for them:

> For if we sin purposely after we have received the knowledge of the truth, there no longer remains a slaughter *offering* for sins, but some fearsome anticipation of judgment, and a fierce fire which is about to consume the opponents. Anyone who has disregarded the Torah of Mosheh dies without compassion on the witness of two or three witnesses. How much worse punishment do you think shall he deserve who has trampled the Son of Elohim underfoot, counted the blood of the covenant by which he was set apart as common, and insulted the Spirit of favour? (Hebrews 10:26-29 ISR)

Reading the last three chapters in Revelation 20-22 is very eye-opening. Here are a few verses from these chapters:

> Blessed *are* those who do his commandments, that

they may have the right to the tree of life, and may enter through the gates into the city. But outside *are* dogs and sorcerers and sexually immoral and murderers and idolaters, and whoever loves and practices a lie. (Revelation 22:14-15 NKJV)

And I saw a great white throne and Him who was sitting on it, from whose face the earth and the heaven fled away, and no place was found for them. And I saw the dead, small and great, standing before the throne, and books were opened. And another book was opened, which is *the Book* of Life. And the dead were judged from what was written in the books, according to their works. And the sea gave up the dead who were in it, and Death and She'ol gave up the dead who were in them. And they were judged, each one according to his works. And Death and She'ol were thrown into the lake of fire. This is the second death. And if anyone was not found written in the Book of Life, he was thrown into the lake of fire. (Revelation 20:11-15 ISR)

The phrase "judged, each one according to his works" means according to our obedience to His commands, which is directly correlated to His Law. It is our enemy's job to trip us up in our walk in caring about our Father's design and even to make us feel we can't follow it, so why try? We dangerously feel we can just take our chances.

Isn't it important to find out what commands show us what is detestable to our Maker? We say we love Him, but do we really care to know what He hates? Our enemy twists the truth in order to turn us against our Heavenly Father to make us uncaring and ignorant. This is exactly how we end up calling evil "good" and good "evil." When reading His Word, our Creator describes the things that are detestable to Him, calling them abominations. It all boils down to whether we really *know* Him—His likes and His dislikes.

Here are a few books in addition to the Law and Prophets where you can do a word search for "abominable/abomination" and see exactly what He hates in Leviticus, Deuteronomy, 1 Kings and 2 Kings, 2 Chronicles, Ezra, Psalms, and Proverbs. He likewise explains what He abhors through the prophets: Isaiah, Jeremiah, Ezekiel, and Malachi. I will only quote a few verses here:

> Do not do so to יהוה your Elohim, for every abomination which יהוה hates they have done to their mighty ones, for they even burn their sons and daughters in the fire to their mighty ones. (Deuteronomy 12:31 ISR)

To kill young children for the sake of idol worship—how dangerously close is this to our practice of killing our unborn babies for the sake of serving ourselves, as society calls it "a woman's right to her body?"

Below is another verse in Proverbs we shouldn't ignore concerning the Law and our prayers:

> One who turns his ear away from listening to the Law, even his prayer is an abomination. (Proverbs 28:9 NASB)

Leviticus chapter 18 gives a list of commands in the Law concerning sexual relationships that He calls abominations. And picking up in verses 24-30, He gives a conclusion for these abominations that He listed before in Leviticus 18:1-23:

> Do not defile yourselves with all these, for by all these the nations are defiled, which I am driving out before you. Thus the land became defiled, therefore I punished it for its crookedness, and the land vomited out its inhabitants. But you, you shall guard My

laws and My right-rulings and not do any of these abominations, the native nor stranger who sojourns among you, because the men of the land who were before you have done all these abominations, and thus the land became defiled, So let not the land vomit you out for defiling it, as it vomited out the nations that were before you. For whoever does any of these abominations, those beings who do them shall be cut off from among their people. And you shall guard My Charge, so as not to do any of these abominable laws which were done before you, so as not to defile yourselves by them. I am יהוה your Elohim. (Leviticus 18:24-30 ISR)

I want you to note several things here. First, notice that our Creator in verse 24 says He does not want His people to defile themselves the way the people that lived in the land before them defiled themselves. It stands to reason that our Creator is saying that it doesn't matter whether these behaviors were practiced by previous people, strangers, or even natives of the land. He is showing us that *all of them are capable of defiling themselves* as well as defiling the land. This is not just a "Jewish" command.

Second, how did the land "vomit" the people out of it? When you read what Yahuweh commanded to be done to these people who occupied the land before them, it wasn't good. They were "vomited out" by being conquered and killed to remove them from the land.

And when יהוה your Elohim gives them over to you, you shall strike them and put them under the ban, completely. Make no covenant with them, and show them no favour. (Deuteronomy 7:2 ISR)

"To put them under the ban completely" means to destroy, to kill them completely.

And you shall know today that יהוה your Elohim is He who is passing over before you as a consuming fire—He does destroy them and subdue them before you. So you shall dispossess them and destroy them quickly, as יהוה has said to you. (Deuteronomy 9:3 ISR)

Third, in verse 29 it says: "For whoever does any of these abominations, those beings shall be cut off from among their people." What do you think *cut off from among their people* means? It very likely means the judgment of death. The following verse speaks of putting to death those who committed adultery, which is also one of the same abominations listed in Leviticus 18 that also declares they will be *cut off from among their people.* See what you think:

> The man who commits adultery with *another* man's wife, *he* who commits adultery with his neighbor's wife, the adulterer and the adulteress, shall surely be put to death. (Leviticus 20:10 NKJV)

Now look at this statement where Yahuweh connects being put to death with being cut off:

> Again, you shall say to the children of Israel: "Whoever of the children of Israel, or of the strangers who dwell in Israel, who gives *any* of his descendants to Molech, he shall surely be put to death. The people of the land shall stone him with stones. I will set My face against that man, and will cut him off from his people, because he has given *some* of his descendants to Molech, to defile My sanctuary and profane My holy name." (Leviticus 20:2-3 NKJV)

"Being cut off," here again, means being put to death. And at the very least, being cut off from the people our Father considers to be "His people" is bad enough. Since we do not live in a

Torah-governed society at this time, we cannot invoke a death penalty for adulterers, yet I know if anyone continues to *defiantly* walk in any sin against the Law, that person will eventually be cut off from being with the people who will live with Yahuweh and His Son forever. The consequences still remain. In the past, I had never paid much attention to that phrase of being cut off from among the people, but now I do.

And in giving their offspring to the pagan deity Molech, the people would burn them in the fire that they built, which was usually constructed at the base or within the structure of this deity's statue. Child sacrifice, murder, and even exploitation, whether mentally, emotionally, or physically harming a child, I strongly believe any and all of these actions will be judged and accounted for in the end.

Look at just these verses showing our Maker's concern for children:

> You are the one who put me together inside my mother's body, and I praise you because of the wonderful way you created me. Everything you do is marvelous! Of this I have no doubt. Nothing about me is hidden from you! I was secretly woven together out of human sight, but with your own eyes you saw my body being formed. Even before I was born, you had written in your book everything about me. Your thoughts are far beyond my understanding, much more than I could ever imagine. (Psalm 139:13-17 CEV)

> See that you do not despise one of these little ones, for I say to you that in the heavens their messengers always see the face of My Father who is in the heavens. (Matthew 18:10 ISR)

Especially concerning children, we have been warned.

I'm not going to rewrite the commandments of the Law concerning sexual sins recorded in Leviticus 18:1-23, as you can easily read them for yourself online or in your copy of the Word. But know these commands of the Law include sexual relations between parents and their children and grandchildren, all the way to sexual relations with aunts and neighbor's wives, as well as having intercourse between men, between women, and between humans and beasts. None of these behaviors are new or liberating as they continue to be practiced to this day. They date back from the time of ancient pagan cultures to even before the time of Noah and are always accompanied with eventual judgment by our Creator, who is jealous for His ways of righteousness.

The New Testament writings even lists these behaviors as "lusts of the flesh" that Paul warns the believers, over and over again, not to fall back into. Paul tells the believers in 1 Corinthians 10:7-8 not to commit the same whoring of the original Israelites, where 23,000 died of a plague in one day as recorded in Numbers 25. In total 24,000 altogether died from Yahuweh's plague because of the whoring and idol worship of Baal Peor. Baal Peor worship continues today, and at the time of the original Israelites was practiced in Moab. Participants are known to engage in all manner of sexual immorality with no restraint.

Do you see how closely the Law is tied to Paul's New Testament teachings? And again, any discussion of our works, whether good or evil, righteous or unrighteous, is defined by the Law. Paul is adamant about the need for leaving behind the sins of the flesh and talks often in his letters about whoring, which is also translated also as sexual immorality. Here I will quote just two of his many writings concerning this:

> Put to death, therefore, the components of your earthly nature: sexual immorality, impurity, lust, evil desires, and greed, which is idolatry. (Colossians 3:5 Berean Study Bible)

Have you noticed how often idolatry, greed, and sexual immorality seem to go hand in hand?

> Do you not know that the unrighteous shall not inherit the reign of Elohim? Do not be deceived. Neither those who whore, nor idolaters, nor adulterers, nor effeminate, nor homosexuals, nor thieves, nor greedy of gain, nor drunkards, nor revilers, nor swindlers shall inherit the reign of Elohim. And such were some of you. But you were washed, but you were set apart, but you were declared right in the Name of the Master יהושע and by the Spirit of our Elohim. (1 Corinthians 6:9-11 ISR)

To our own demise, we pridefully continue to demand acceptance of some of these behaviors in our own societies today. But sin never sits still; it keeps on moving, edging us further and further away from our Creator and His protection, His righteousness, and from our inheritance with Him.

As you can see, Paul doesn't make excuses for those feeling stuck in sin. He expects us to believe that sins of all kinds are to be overcome through the power of washing that comes in the Name of the Master Yahushua. This powerful forgiveness and overcoming is a miracle to all who believe and allow themselves to be transformed by His power and His Spirit. Our Creator is a mighty Elohim, and there is nothing too hard for Him!

So taking Him at His Word, whether our flesh likes it or not is what He is after—our trust and our allegiance, not our defiance. The reward of our allegiance is great, and the curse of defiance is just as great. It is the behaviors we each choose in this life that determine our destiny in the next.

Now, back to the commandments. And this is a part of the Ten Commandments in the Law that is so often overlooked. See the curse that is stated at the end of verse 5:

> You do not make for yourself a carved image, or

any likeness of that which is in the heavens above, or which is in the earth beneath, or which is in the waters under the earth, you do not bow down to them nor serve them. For I, יהוה your Elohim am a jealous El, visiting the crookedness of the fathers on the children to the third and fourth generations of those who hate Me. (Exodus 20:4-5 ISR)

We too quickly think, "Well, I don't make carved images, and I surely don't *hate* my Heavenly Father," so I'm free of any curses that may be caused by idolatry. The word *hate* in Hebrew can also mean simply to *love less*—to love Him less than we love something or someone else does equal idolatry in our Father's eyes! Remember His jealousy. He says to love Him with *all* our heart, soul, and strength—with *all our being*—loving Him first before ourselves, before anyone or anything else.

And remember what Paul says amounts to idolatry in Colossians 3:5 that I just quoted for you above? Idolatry is connected to sexual immorality, impurity, lust, evil desires, and greed. And if you need further evidence, look at the following verses:

...because, although they knew Elohim, they did not esteem Him as Elohim, nor gave thanks, but became vain in their reasonings, and their undiscerning heart was darkened. Claiming to be wise, they became fools, and changed the esteem of the incorruptible Elohim into the likeness of an image of corruptible man, and of birds and of four-footed beasts and of reptiles. Therefore Elohim gave them up to uncleanness in the lust of their hearts, to disrespect their bodies among themselves. (Romans 1:21-24 ISR)

When we do not give our Creator thanks and the esteem He deserves for *who* He is and what He has done, we become *vain* in our reasonings which is Greek Strong's #3152 *mataios*, meaning to render (passively, become) foolish, i.e., (morally) wicked or (specially) idolatrous—to become vain.

Changed the esteem of the incorruptible Elohim into the likeness of an image of corruptible man—how do you think we do this today? We give honor and praise to ourselves and the things that we have done and created more than we give our esteem of honor and praise to our Creator. He does not receive the honor and praise He deserves each and every day that we ignore Him and do not rely on Him but instead rely on ourselves and our own strength. He is very, very serious about being #1 in our lives! So, the uncleanness in the lust of our hearts leads to disrespecting our bodies, and we exchange indecencies with each other rather than relationships grounded in righteous living before our Creator. Keep reading the rest of Romans chapter 1 in your copy of His Word and read through to the last verse of Romans 1:32. You will see what all this means even more clearly.

Idolatry in any form leads to curses to the third and fourth generations, as we have already noted in the very first two laws of the Ten Commandments.

There is not one family that does not have generational curses in its previous generations. So knowing that we can receive curses from three and four generations back, as well as pass them on to our descendants to the third and fourth generation, how do we then stop these curses? I think you know the answer already. We have inherited the curse of sin from Adam, which puts all of us in the position that "all have sinned and fall short of the esteem of Yahuweh." Our inherited carnal nature is to sin, yet we are commanded to overcome, and this includes not only overcoming our nature to sin but to overcome the specific sins we have inherited from our ancestors as well as sins that we have personally opened the door to in our lives. How do we stop all this?

1. You must start with faith and repentance in Yahushua Messiah for the cleansing of your conscience through His blood sacrifice, which also forgives and cleanses you from all *past* sins. Only in this way can you receive the power, knowledge, and prompting of the Set-apart Spirit of Truth in order to obey Yahuweh's commands. Only in this way can you overcome sin and begin to love and please Him—His way. This means that you have a circumcised heart (a heart in which the outer covering is symbolically cut away so that one can feel), in order to love your Creator with all your being. Remember Deuteronomy 30:6. This is the heart of the matter.

2. You must continue to be led by your Creator and Heavenly Father in His commands through His Set-apart Spirit and not by men. While it is possible for you to be encouraged and even instructed by others, it is also possible to blindly follow the leading of other human beings. This is dangerous!

3. Stay in a state of humble prayer (communication of requests, praise, and thankfulness to Yahuweh in His Son's name, Yahushua) as Paul admonishes in Ephesians 6:18 ISR "praying at all times, with all prayer and supplication in the Spirit, watching in all perseverance and supplication for all the set-apart ones." (Also see Philippians 4:6.)

4. And then you need to gather with other believers who are seeking the truth of the Scriptures and learning to walk in His commandments. There are many people all over the world now who are waking up to the fact that our Creator's Law has not been abolished, and who also know it's not okay for man to have changed even the timing of the appointed gathering of the Sabbath from the seventh day to the first day of the week.

So, now let's return to the Ten Commandments and look at the last six, because we have already discussed the first four commandments through previous chapters (2 and 3) as well as earlier in this chapter:

> [12] Respect your father and your mother, so that your days are prolonged upon the soil which יהוה your Elohim is giving you.
>
> [13] You do not murder.
>
> [14] You do not commit adultery.
>
> [15] You do not steal.
>
> [16] You do not bear false witness against your neighbour.
>
> [17] You do not covet your neighbour's house, you do not covet your neighbour's wife, nor his male servant, nor his female servant, nor his ox, nor his donkey, or whatever belongs to your neighbour. (Exodus 20:12-17 ISR)

We easily see these last six laws in the Ten Commandments are still relevant today.

So knowing all of this, why are many continuing to teach and preach lawlessness? Remember the areas I discussed in the previous chapter that steer us away from our obedience? We are all guilty of picking and choosing which commands to keep, but this does not justify our actions nor excuse ignoring our Maker's design in His eyes. We don't like crucifying the flesh, especially when it comes to sex and food; it's easier to say *the Law has been abolished and we can now do what we want.* His food commands are discussed in the next chapters, and we've already discussed some of the sexual relation laws.

We must be careful in how we live, and especially in how

we lead and teach others to live. Christian leaders will be held no less responsible than the religious leaders in biblical times. The following verses are harsh, but know that His prophecies are often cyclical—they come back around. The words of the following prophets, Jeremiah, Isaiah, and Ezekiel, speak not only for a time that was to come and was fulfilled in ancient Israel, but they also prophesy of what we are seeing now and what is to come for us and future generations.

Jeremiah chapter 23 starts by saying "woe to the shepherds." Then later, Yahuweh reprimands the people as well as the false prophets and shepherds who were supposed to be feeding truth to Yahuweh's flocks, but instead spoke their own words.

> "Woe to the shepherds destroying and scattering the sheep of My pasture!" declares יהוה. Therefore thus said יהוה Elohim of Yisra'el against the shepherds who feed My people, "You have scattered My flock, driven them away, and have not tended them. See, I am punishing you for the evil of your deeds," declares יהוה. "Therefore I shall gather the remnant of my flock out of all the lands where I have driven them, and shall bring them back to their fold. And they shall bear and increase. And I shall raise up shepherds over them, and they shall feed them. And they shall fear no more, nor be discouraged, nor shall they be lacking," declares יהוה. "See, the days are coming," declares יהוה, "when I shall raise for Dawid a Branch of righteousness, and a Sovereign shall reign and act wisely, and shall do right-ruling and righteousness in the earth. In His days Yehudah shall be saved, and Yisra'el dwell safely. And this is His Name whereby He shall be called: 'יהוה our Righteousness.' Therefore, see, the days are coming," declares יהוה, when they shall say no more 'As יהוה

lives who brought up the children of Yisra'el out of the land of Mitsrayim.' but, 'As יהוה lives who brought up and led the seed of the house of Yisra'el out of the land of the north and from all the lands where I had driven them.' And they shall dwell on their own soil." (Jeremiah 23:1-8 ISR)

"They keep on saying to those who despise Me, ' יהוה has said you shall have peace.' And to all who walk according to the stubbornness of their own heart *they* say, 'No evil comes upon you.' " (Jeremiah 23:17 ISR)

"But if they had stood in My counsel, then they would have let My people hear My Words, and they would have turned them from their evil way and from the evil of their deeds. (Jeremiah 23:22 ISR)

"As for the prophet and the priest and the people who say, 'The message of יהוה,' I shall punish that man and his house. This is what each one says to his neighbour, and each one to his brother, 'What has יהוה answered?' and 'What has יהוה spoken?' But the message of יהוה you no longer remember! For every man's message is his own word, for you have changed the Words of the living Elohim יהוה of hosts, our Elohim! (Jeremiah 23:34-36 ISR)

Do you see how this is where we are at today in forgetting the Word, the Torah of our Elohim, and the commands that we *can* keep?

Also Isaiah records Yahuweh speaking again his warning against the shepherds with even stronger words:

His watchmen are blind, all of them, they have not known. All of them are dumb dogs, unable to bark, dreaming, lying down, loving to slumber. And the dogs have a strong appetite, they never have enough. And they are shepherds! They have not known understanding. All of them look to their own way, every one for his own gain, from his own end, *saying*, "Come, let me bring wine and fill ourselves with strong drink. And tomorrow shall be as today, even much greater." (Isaiah 56:10-12 ISR)

I know this sounds harsh, but think about it. When we deny the Words of our Creator that are designed to be taught, preached, and lived, but we replace them with our own words of expectation of peace, protection, and provision while leaving out the warnings and disregarding His Law, then our words have become the deceit of strong wine. I pray that those reading this book who are in the position of shepherding others have already grasped the gravity of Isaiah's words.

We must be very careful to examine what we are teaching, especially to the new believer. Are we setting him or her up for failure as well as our own selves for condemnation and judgment?

Here is how we lead others in the wrong direction:

The "church" does an excellent job in delivering the message that *we are sinners* and in need of a Savior. Yet far too many churches still teach the need to repent of sins that are against a Law that they say has been abolished. How confusing is this? Where are the guidelines for walking as our Messiah walked in newness of life? How are we supposed to know what sin is without the Law? How are we supposed to know how to please our Heavenly Father, to be perfect (complete) as He is perfect? (Deuteronomy 18:13, Matthew 5:48)

I have also heard that there are some religious leaders who teach that the "moral laws" are still viable and never went away, while disregarding the laws that they believe were abolished and are not included in their definition of what constitutes the "moral laws." But even with that being said, I ask, how do you sort out which laws fall into the "moral" category and which ones do not? Who gets to decide?

I believe, the Law, *all of it*, is still in place just as Yahushua said in Matthew 5:17-18, even though there are commands we cannot complete at this time.

We must prayerfully and fearfully read our Maker's commandments in the Law and Prophets in addition to reading the gospel accounts, including the book of Acts, to see how our Messiah, the apostles, and Paul lived out Yahuweh's commandments. And then we must follow their example.

It is interesting, as you read the book of Acts, to see the instances in which both Paul and Stephen defended their loyal adherence to the Law when being accused of acting otherwise. See Acts chapter 6 and 7 for the story of Stephen's defense of the Law as he was being accused by the so-called "Freedmen," as well as Acts 25:8.

If we seek His guidance on how to incorporate the commands we *are* able to do into our own lives, no matter how small or big, this is what our Heavenly Father is after in being our guide over every aspect of our lives, rather than us guiding ourselves. As you read on through the remaining chapters, you will understand even more of what I'm talking about here.

Some of you have already begun to keep His Sabbaths that include the seventh-day Sabbaths as well as the annual feast days, knowing that they are vital even though there are many other laws we cannot keep.

In conclusion, I want to ask again: *what if you found out there are many commands you cannot complete*? Will you ignore those commands that you know you can keep but are just not willing to crucify the flesh for? Or will you keep reading His word, prayerfully searching for the commands that you *can* complete to know and to obey your Maker, to walk as His Son walked, steering away from sin by using His Law as your guide as He always intended?

CHAPTER 9

What if you found out there is even a design for how we are to dress?

WITH THE REALIZATION THAT I must obey what He has revealed, in the manner that He commands, whether it is small or great, dividing or uniting, easy or difficult, self-sacrificing or not, I began to follow my Messiah, walking as He walked, and to die daily to my flesh (my own desires). It all began when I had to get all the Christmas stuff out of the house that night as described in Chapter 1. Then as described in Chapter 2, I, along with my husband and my mother, began to see it's not that hard to refrain from our own pleasures on the Sabbath and to guard it in the way His Scriptures say we are to do. Three years later, I found another command that I was not looking for. I realized it's not that hard to refrain from wearing men's clothes.

What?

> A woman must not wear men's clothing, nor a man wear women's clothing, for the Lord your God detests anyone who does this. (Deuteronomy 22:5 NIV)

At first, I did not like this verse at all! I loved my comfortable blue jeans. I worked outside painting houses with Kevin and climbing ladders. I climbed over fences to feed animals. And I'm just more comfortable in jeans. I had to wrestle with this command and reason it out as I thought: *Men wear "men's pants" and women wear "women's pants," so I can still wear pants, right?* But in knowing that my Heavenly Father is very specific and detailed in all He creates and commands, He must have a very good reason for trying to make a clear distinction between men and women. Did He not miraculously and with intent form us in our mother's womb?

Then I thought maybe He *does* mean for women not to wear pants. Still wrestling with my own desires, I thought of the reality shows of two very large families where the mothers and all their daughters wear dresses and skirts, and even play sports, repair cars, and do carpentry in skirts, sometimes with leggings underneath. I wondered why they appeared to be so consistent in their dress code, then realized it's probably out of modesty. But could it also be because they found this command in the Scriptures like I did?

I went back and forth in trying to figure out what I should do. I knew my Creator was definitely detailed in all His creations. Look at the flowers and how they are dressed. Then I thought about many of the bathroom signs that still remain in public areas where, if you couldn't read, you would still know which restroom is the men's and which restroom is the women's because the women's sign displays a figure wearing a dress and the men's sign does not. And if a restroom is advertised as "gender neutral," I've still seen the same signs beside the door with both a figure in a dress and a figure not in a dress. The dress symbol is still there. I also thought about our tendencies as humans to test our boundaries, to push against the goads, to act proudly and defiantly in pushing the limits even in some of the seemingly small areas of expressing ourselves, such as in "cross dressing." So, it made sense that our Creator would care about how He wants us to dress.

Is this asking too much of me? Am I not supposed to lay down my life and the way that I want to live it for my Messiah's sake?

> Or do you not know that your body is the Dwelling Place of the Set-apart Spirit who is in you, which you have from Elohim, and you are not your own? For you were bought with a price, therefore esteem Elohim in your body and in your spirit, which are of Elohim. (1 Corinthians 6:19-20 ISR)

I believe these verses are telling me to honor my Heavenly Father and His Son in everything I do, even in the details, while I'm in this earthly body. So I went to my closet and removed all my jeans and pants and got them out of the house. I knew that if I left them there, I would be tempted to wear them. I replaced them with skirts, especially several denim skirts and jumpers, from secondhand stores. I then had a few "everyday" work skirts as well as some "special occasion" skirts. As I sit and write this chapter, I remember something about my dear Grandmother Bane (my daddy's mother) that I had forgotten. I do not recall ever seeing my grandmother in pants of any kind, whether in person or in photos. I even asked my mother if she could recall having ever seen her mother-in-law in pants or slacks. Mother shook her head and said, "No."

I was twelve years old when Grandmother Bane died in 1972. She was 79 years old, and I relish the many memories I have of spending time with her on her East Texas farm, using her kitchen forks to dig potatoes out of the hot, red, East Texas dirt. She made me wear a cotton bonnet when we went to her garden, and I still have it to this day. I recall getting up early every morning, before everyone else, and dressing as we crouched by the little gas heater in her room, and the smell of fresh-perked coffee drifting in from that old farmhouse kitchen. I can still see her thin, strong fingers mixing the dough from the well of flour she had made in the center of the bowl, preparing to make biscuits. During the day, I helped her collect eggs from the two-story barn steps where the chickens liked to lay. We hung clothes on the line beside the house, and I don't remember ever seeing a clothes dryer in her house. In the evenings, we would sit around my grandparents' makeshift bedroom/family room, shelling pecans and black-eyed peas. She did all these things and more, in her simple, cotton-print work dresses with three-quarter-length sleeves and a thin, matching print belt. These are some of my most treasured memories.

Well, coming back from memory lane, let's look at something else I noticed in Deuteronomy 22:5 and the words that different translations use. Note the ending word that states men wearing women's clothes and women wearing men's clothes is an "abomination" to our Heavenly Father. This is another one of those laws in which He describes certain behaviors as abominable, like we discussed in the previous chapters.

Note: I do not like quoting translations that use "God and LORD" for our Heavenly Father and His Son, as I stated back in Chapter 3, but to emphasize the word "abomination," I chose to use them here.

> A woman shall not wear a man's clothing, nor shall a man put on women's clothing; for whoever does these things is an abomination to the LORD your God. (Deuteronomy 22:5 NASB)

> A woman shall not wear anything that pertains to a man, nor shall a man put on a woman's garment, for all who do so are an abomination to the LORD your God. (Deuteronomy 22:5 NKJV)

Why would just my choice of clothing make Him feel this

way? Is He really that serious? I do claim to love Him and know that if I want His blessings and protection, I must find out what pleases Him and obey Him even when these things are not "abominable" to me. So now, despite what anyone else says or thinks, I have not worn pants or blue jeans for more than six years. It is not too hard on me, or beneath me, to do this for Him as I continue on my quest to know His heart.

Remember, we are responsible for how we use the knowledge we have been given as He reveals His word to each of us. Knowing and then choosing to ignore His commands, even the seemingly unimportant ones, is deliberate sin of which the writer of Hebrews gives us a clear warning:

> If we deliberately keep on sinning after we have received the knowledge of the truth, no sacrifice for sins is left. (Hebrew 10:26 NIV)

And this law below is connected to the above verse:

> But the being who does *whatever* defiantly, whether he is native or a stranger, he reviles יהוה, and that being shall be cut off from among his people. Because he has despised the word of יהוה, and broken His command, that being shall certainly be cut off, his crookedness is upon him. (Numbers 15:30-31 ISR)

> So whoever knows the right thing to do and fails to do it, for him it is sin. (James 4:17, ESV)

Also look at the words of our Messiah concerning this parable:

> And that servant who knew his master's will but did not get ready or act according to his will, will receive a severe beating. (Luke 12:47, ESV)

I do not think this literally means to receive a beating, but this parable *is* teaching a principle that to know the Father's will and to refuse to do it is serious. A reverent fear of our Creator is what He expects of us in order to be set-apart from the rest of the world:

> Because this is the covenant that I shall make with the house of Yisra'el after those days, says יהוה, giving My laws in their mind, and I shall write them on their hearts, and I shall be their Elohim, and they shall be My people. (Hebrews 8:10 ISR)

> "And I shall give them one heart, and put a new spirit within you. And I shall take the stony heart out of their flesh, and give them a heart of flesh, so that they walk in My laws, and guard My right-rulings, and shall do them. And they shall be My people and I shall be their Elohim. But to those whose hearts walk after the heart of their disgusting *matters* and their abominations, I shall recompense their deeds on their own heads," declares the Master יהוה. (Ezekiel 11:19-21 ISR)

> "But this word I did command them, saying, Obey My voice, and I shall be your Elohim, and you be My people. And walk in all the ways that I have commanded you, so that it be well with you." (Jeremiah 7:23 ISR)

> And I heard a loud voice from the heaven saying, "See, the Booth of Elohim is with men, and He shall dwell with them, and they shall be His people, and Elohim Himself shall be with them and be their Elohim." (Revelation 21:3 ISR)

He will not and cannot live with a people who have gone their own way, doing the things that He considers wrong and even abominable. It takes our obedience to His commands as much as it takes trusting in the forgiveness of His Son—it takes both.

We get to decide in this life if we're going to search for how to please Him, to obey the commands that we can complete in spite of the ones we found we cannot complete, in order to be His set-apart people.

> For you are a set-apart people to יהוה your Elohim,
> and יהוה has chosen you to be a people for Himself,
> a treasured possession above all the peoples who are
> on the face of the earth. (Deuteronomy 14:2 ISR)

CHAPTER 10

*What if you found out there are commands
for what our Maker considers is food?*

I T IS INTERESTING HOW WE ended the previous chapter
with Deuteronomy 14:2, Yahuweh's declaration about His
people being set-apart, as the very next verse in this same
chapter of Deuteronomy says:

> Do not eat whatever is abominable. These are the
> living creatures which you do eat: ox, sheep, and
> goat, deer, and gazelle, and roebuck, and wild goat,
> and mountain goat, and antelope, and mountain
> sheep. And every beast that has a split hoof divided
> in two, chewing the cud, among the beasts, you do
> eat. But of those chewing the cud or those having a
> split hoof completely divided, you do not eat, such
> as these: the camel, and the hare, and the rabbit,
> for they chew the cud but do not have a split hoof,
> they are unclean for you. And the pig is unclean for
> you, because it has a split hoof, but does not chew
> the cud. You do not eat their flesh or touch their
> dead carcasses. These you do eat of all that are in the
> waters: all that have fins and scales you do eat. And
> whatever does not have fins and scales you do not

eat, it is unclean for you. Any clean bird you do eat, but these you do not eat: the eagle, and the vulture, and the black vulture, and red kite, and the falcon, and the buzzard after their kinds, and every raven after its kind, and the ostrich, and the nighthawk, and the seagull, and the hawk after their kinds, the little owl, and the great owl, and the white owl, and the pelican, and the carrion vulture, and the fisher owl, and the stork, and the heron after its kind, and the hoopoe and the bat. And every creeping *insect* that flies is unclean for you, they are not eaten. Any clean bird you do eat. (Deuteronomy 14:3-20 ISR)

This is another commandment we were never taught. When we realized this was an area in our lives we needed to bring under our Father's leadership, it was quite a challenge to explain why Kevin suddenly stopped eating ham. Everyone in our family knew of his love for baked ham. As soon as he read Deuteronomy 14:3-20 and Leviticus 11:1-47, he saw that our Creator designed and defined exactly what He considers to be *food* for us and Kevin immediately dropped from his diet pork and shellfish, as well as other water creatures that were created to clean the waterways and oceans. I was shocked! You know how a wife will often watch over the food her husband eats, trying to get him to eat healthier and so forth? I didn't have anything to do with this change! Kevin's conviction after reading these scriptures was totally all his own, as it should be.

The biological makeup of a pig and its eating habits is an interesting study, especially if you want to know what "clean eating" really is. Just because a pig is raised organic, it doesn't make eating pork *clean* as the advertisers want us to believe. Yahuweh's details are in His Word, and now, with the internet at our fingertips, it's easy to research the science and historical precedence of the consequences of mankind's choices. For health reasons alone, it would be worth our time to look at the research that documents what the consumption of pork and other unclean creatures can do to the human body.

Below are three websites I found easily by doing an internet search for "pigs are abominable to eat scientifically."

**http://amazinghealth.com/
AH-health-unclean-animals-pig-fish-mammals**

**https://www.offthegridnews.com/off-grid-foods/gods-
dietary-laws-why-pigs-crabs-and-lobstersare-bad-for-you/**

**http://www.uncleanfoodsdietarylaws.com/
unclean_foods_dietary_laws.html**

When you think of how Yahuweh tells us not to eat buzzards or vultures, it's easy to see why. But it's a little harder to see why we shouldn't consume other things we have grown accustomed to eating, even though they were never considered food by our Creator. And the cooking shows that I love to watch, which now have such a big push for consuming bacon, make their recipes look so good! We really never stopped to think all those years we ate oysters, crab, lobster, and shrimp, that they are filters of toxins that clean up the oceans and waterways by design. The same is true about the intended function of vultures, pigs, hawks, and buzzards. They were also created to be "cleaner uppers" of the land. And a catfish doesn't have scales; Yahuweh states both fins and scales are needed for a fish to be considered food. My Mom had always said catfish had a taste of dirt to it. At the time, I thought she was just being picky. Then when I learned that catfish are bottom dwellers, it made sense why they tasted like dirt. It also makes sense now why oysters can make you so sick.

What we eat as consumers is big business, but we are beginning to wise up in finding out about the processing, chemicals, and pesticides that we have been led to believe are harmless. So why should we believe that certain creatures are food when they really aren't? Our Creator obviously knows more than we do and cares about every aspect of our lives from the words we say, to how we dress, to what we eat. Is it too much for Him to ask of me to learn to eat the way He designed?

It is not.

And I don't believe Yahushua, dying for our sins, took away the law for what we are supposed to eat and not eat. That would be like saying our Maker has changed His mind about His design. Remember the following verse I quoted at the beginning of this chapter?

> Do not eat whatever is abominable. (Deuteronomy 14:3 ISR)

Has He really changed what He considers detestable, thus changing His definition of what is righteous and what is not?

It all goes back to three basics: humility, fear, and love. We either humbly have the fear of our Creator and love Him enough that we dare not go against Him even in the seemingly insignificant matters such as our food choices—or we do not.

CHAPTER 11

What if you found out that accepting the gift
of salvation does not make you a Christian?

But He answered and said, "I was sent only to the
lost sheep of the house of Israel." (Matthew 15:24
NASB)

HY WOULD OUR MESSIAH SAY such a thing since
we know that He came to save the whole world?
You may be asking, what do the lost sheep of Israel
have to do with becoming a Christian? Who are the lost sheep of
the house of Israel? What does this mean?

I had always been very proud of identifying myself as a
Christian, yet I had never stopped to wonder where this name
came from. So again, I researched, first in my *Strong's Concor-*
dance under the words "Christian/Christians," and found that
this term was only used three times in the KJV in Acts 11:26
and 26:28, and in 1 Peter 4:16. As I read these verses, I saw that
nowhere in all of the New Testament writings did our Messiah
ever describe His followers as Christians. Nor did He predict or
warn His followers that they would be called by this name. Peter
was the only disciple to use this term, and he only used it once.

The other two occurrences of the word "Christian" in the KJV were used by the Gentiles in Antioch as they scornfully labeled believers "followers of Messiah." The ISR translation in both Acts 11:26 and 26:28 uses the term "messianist" instead of "Christian."

As noted earlier in Chapter 3 of this book, the word "Christ" or "Christos" is very closely related to the pagan deity Osiris, who was worshipped as "Chrestos," meaning "good." C. J. Koster, in his book *Come Out of Her, My People*, also states that "Chrestos" was a common Greek proper name meaning "good."

I also read a very interesting article online with the title, "Should We Call Ourselves a Christian?" by Richard Anthony. It confirmed some of the research I had already done in using my *Strong's Concordance* and Scriptures, saying that the name or identification of the word "Christian" did not come from the Father or from His Son but originated with Gentiles.

Again, I truly believe that we, His people, are to be defined by who and what He says we are. Now look at the following verses for how the Apostle Paul defines believers in Messiah:

> Therefore remember that you, once nations in the flesh, who are called 'the uncircumcision' by what is called 'the circumcision' made in the flesh by hands, that at that time you were without Messiah, excluded from the citizenship of Yisra'el and strangers from the covenants of promise, having no expectation and without Elohim in the world. But now in Messiah יהושע you who once were far off have been brought near by the blood of the Messiah. (Ephesians 2:11-13 ISR)
>
> So then you are no longer strangers and foreigners, but fellow citizens of the set-apart ones and members of the household of Elohim. (Ephesians 2:19 ISR)

Therefore, recognize that it is those who are of faith who are sons of Abraham. (Galatians 3:7 NASB)

We can see that through the Messiah, our Heavenly Father also refers to the lost sheep of Israel in Ezekiel 34 as being the sheep He is going to gather from all the places that He has scattered them. This is future prophecy and has not happened yet. The following verse at the end of chapter 34 shows that Yahuweh calls His end-time people "the house of Yisra'el." Please take the time to read the whole chapter of Ezekiel 34.

'And they shall know that I, יהוה their Elohim, am with them, and that they, the house of Yisra'el, are My people,' declares the Master יהוה. (Ezekiel 34:30 ISR)

The nations to be co-heirs, united in the same body, and partakers together in the promise in Messiah through the Good News. (Ephesians 3:6 ISR)

Paul says that new believers who were once nations (Gentiles) are now "co-heirs" with the (Jews) who also choose to become believers in Messiah. Both are made *one* in the spiritual citizenship of Yisra'el. Scripture does not say that both become Christians. This citizenship, heirship, is also backed again by Paul in Galatians:

And if you are of Messiah, then you are seed of Abraham, and heirs according to promise. (Galatians 3:29 ISR)

When we understand this, then we can identify and claim Yahuweh's promises and commands for His people from the beginning. We are not outsiders any longer! We, once Gentiles, are no longer strangers to the promises, provisions, and instructions of our Heavenly Father as *His people*.

Also when we understand that we become citizens of Israel

(Yahweh's chosen people that He calls "Israel"), the words in Genesis to Revelation begin to open up and reveal some long-oppressed truths of how to really be "His chosen people." Knowing these truths, we can better identify with our Creator and His words to His people. Remember that His words are forever and His righteousness never changes. Identity is always a major area in which our enemy chooses to deceive us.

In summary, I have learned that in order to be called "His," we must take Ephesians 2:19 seriously. We are grafted into the citizenship of Israel through the redeeming blood of our Messiah, when we turn back (repent) from our evil ways (our sins), asking for forgiveness. And then we learn to walk in newness of life (without sin) by following His righteousness, which is His commands (Laws) through the power of the Set-apart Spirit. Now the words of my Messiah make sense to me when I read what He said in Matthew 15:24 KJV that "I am not sent but unto the lost sheep of the house of Israel."

Knowing this truth, I can now claim all the promises of the children of Israel, but also know that the Laws for living and loving given to His people are mine too! And they are not a heavy burden! This is how I now walk, no longer identifying myself as a Christian but as a follower of my Messiah and a citizen of Israel that Yahuweh calls *His people.*

CHAPTER 12
What if you found out the Rapture is just a theory?

I WAS GOING TO LEAVE THIS chapter out of this particular book because of all the other material that I knew needed to be covered, yet the Set-apart Spirit kept prompting me to leave it in. I kept thinking, "Why is it important to know whether the rapture is scriptural? Does it really matter?" Then I realized how many believers are banking on being spared the events of the Tribulation, who will not be prepared if the rapture truly is a theory.

What I am talking about is the thought that believers will be gathered or "raptured" before the terrible days of distress known as the Great Tribulation spoken of in Matthew 24 and in the books of Revelation and Daniel. It will be an unprecedented time when Yahuweh will pour out his wrath on the earth while Satan wars against Him and His people. The beast and the anti-messiah will have control of the world and its leaders. Allegiance to them will be demanded. And for those who refuse, persecution and/or death will result.

Not realizing all of this, I can remember as a very young child having a deep longing to be present when my Savior returns. I do believe our Heavenly Father speaks very simply and clearly to children, and more often than not, we grow up and grow away from hearing His still, small voice. I've never lost that thought but now know more about what has to take place before our Messiah returns. For those living during this time, it's going to take the supernatural power of the Set-apart Spirit to endure the trials of the Tribulation. I see more and more evidence in the Scriptures that points to believers being present during the Tribulation years and then those who are still alive being gathered at the return of our Messiah, which is *after* the Tribulation. Look at the following verses. I'll start in Matthew 24 toward the end of the chapter, but it is important for you to start from the first verse and read through it to the end several times in your own copy of the Word:

> And unless those days were shortened, no flesh would be saved; but for the elect's sake those days will be shortened. (Matthew 24:22 NKJV)

This verse is what I discussed one time with my pastor in that I didn't really believe in a rapture (meaning a pre-tribulation gathering of His people). Do you see what I mean? Why would the time need to be shortened if the elect were already raptured? The word "elect" here is Strong's G1588: "*eklektous,*" meaning "chosen," and is used twenty-three times in the Greek concordance of the KJV. But I want to stop right here and make it very clear that in looking at the word "chosen" in any of the verses in Scripture, I do not advocate for the thinking that certain people are chosen from the beginning of creation (predestined) to receive salvation and others not. This stance takes away our free-will choice to become a believer or not. Our Creator came for all mankind (John 3:17), wishing that no one be left out of His Kingdom, but that all would come to repentance (2 Peter 3:9). He gives that free-will decision to each of us. He did, however, plan for all who will repent and believe to receive salvation through His Son. And a definite characteristic of who these people will be is that they will choose to be humble or *poor in spirit.*

Listen, my beloved brothers: Has Elohim not chosen

the poor of this world, rich in belief and heirs of the reign which He promised to those who love Him? (James 2:5 ISR).

The words in this one verse explain so much! I want to reiterate them: "chosen the poor"; "rich in belief"; "promised to those who love Him"—all of these concepts are thematic throughout the entire Word. He saves those who are poor, which does not mean poor in a negative sense. But, *poor in spirit* means the absence of self-pride that keeps us from *humbly* accepting the gift of the Son and from following the commands of the Father. You cannot be rich in belief and remain prideful. It's the poor in spirit who know their need for a Savior and are humble enough to admit it. It's the poor in spirit who inherit the kingdom of heaven (Matthew 5:3 and Luke 6:20) and get to be with Him forever. The poor in spirit love Him, which by definition means to keep His commands (1John 5:3). Just do a word search for all the verses that contain "pride/prideful." You will get a clear picture of the difference between pride and humility and know that these free-will choices make a difference, especially during the final years of tribulation just before the return of Yahushua.

Notice the words "after" and "Then" in the following verse:

Immediately after the tribulation of those days the sun will be darkened, and the moon will not give its light; the stars will fall from heaven, and the powers of the heavens will be shaken. Then the sign of the Son of Man will appear in heaven, and then all the tribes of the earth will mourn, and they will see the Son of Man coming on the clouds of heaven with power and great glory. And He will send His angels with a great sound of a trumpet, and they will gather together His elect from the four winds, from one end of heaven to the other. (Matthew 24:29-31 NKJV)

Paul even writes of those who will be "left over" at the coming of the Messiah. Read the following verses very carefully, noticing the time frame in which our Messiah gathers those who are living right up until His return. The word "caught away" is popularly taught as "rapture" today, yet it is fondly (but mistakenly) thought of as a pre-tribulation gathering of our Messiah. They miss the word "then" in verse 17:

> Now, brothers, we do not wish you to be ignorant concerning those who have fallen asleep, lest you be sad as others who have no expectation. For if we believe that יהושע died and rose again, so also Elohim shall bring with Him those who sleep in יהושע. For this we say to you by the word of the Master, that we, the living who are left over at the coming of the Master shall in no way go before those who are asleep. Because the Master Himself shall come down from heaven with a shout, with the voice of a chief messenger, and with the trumpet of Elohim, and the dead in Messiah shall rise first. Then we, the living who are left over, shall be caught away together with them in the clouds to meet the Master in the air—and so we shall always be with the Master. So, then, encourage one another with these words. (1 Thessalonians 4:13-18 ISR)

Here is where I want you to think of something as well. In the above verses the Messiah is coming down and the dead in Him, as well as the living who were left over, are rising to meet Him in the air. Why is He coming down? Is it not also to set up His earthly Kingdom but first to war against the beast and the false prophet (Revelation 19:19-21)? He is also gathering His people at this time to be an army with Him to fight against the beast, the false prophet, and their followers. This is why the nations are mourning in Matthew 24. They realize they are doomed and about to do battle with the Messiah and His army. We are so focused on getting off this earth that we think we automatically end up in heaven to stay. This was never the plan. When you read the last three chapters of Revelation (19-21), our Messiah comes back to live on earth with us for a thousand years. Then His Father comes down to the new earth, bringing the new Jerusalem with Him in order to dwell there.

As I was researching for this chapter, I came across still others who try to say the believers who are present during the Tribulation years are only those who were saved during that time period and that all previous believers were raptured and taken up to heaven before the time of the Tribulation. While I pray that there will be many saved even during this horrible time, it will not be easy for them to do so, and many will actually curse Yahuweh during the Tribulation because of the horrible events taking place. See Revelation 16:9-11 and 21.

Examining further in Revelation 13 we see that believers are called in different translations *saints*, *Holy ones*, *God's people* and *set-apart ones*. They are present on the earth during the Tribulation:

> And they worshipped the dragon who gave authority to the beast. And they worshipped the beast, saying, "Who is like the beast? Who is able to fight with him?" And he was given a mouth speaking great *matters* and blasphemies, and he was given authority to do so forty-two months. And he opened his mouth in blasphemies against Elohim, to blaspheme His Name, and His Tent, and those dwelling in the heaven. And it was given to him to fight with the set-apart ones and to overcome them. And authority was given to him over every tribe and tongue and nation. And all those dwelling on the earth, whose names have not been written in the Book of Life of the slain Lamb, from the foundation of the world

shall worship him. If anyone has an ear, let him hear. He who brings into captivity shall go into captivity, he who kills with the sword has to be killed with the sword, Here is the endurance and the belief of the set-apart ones. (Revelation 13:4-10 ISR)

As you can see, the beast is fighting with the set-apart ones in order to overcome them. Yet their endurance is never giving in to the beast, even if it means being brought into captivity or killed. But remember that not all are killed according to the previous verse I quoted, where Paul says, "then we the *living* who are left over," meaning those believers who are still alive at the coming of the Messiah.

As you read further down in the same chapter of Revelation 13 you will get to another statement about those set-apart ones who are chosen to die:

And it was given to him to give breath to the image of the beast, so that the image of the beast would even speak and cause all who do not worship the image of the beast to be killed. (Revelation 13:15 NASB).

But the reward of these set-apart ones is far greater than their trials or their death! They are called *blessed*!

And I saw thrones—and they sat on them, and judgment was given to them—and the lives of those who had been beheaded because of the witness they bore to יהושע and because of the Word of Elohim, and who did not worship the beast, nor his image, and who did not receive his mark upon their foreheads or upon their hands. And they lived and reigned with Messiah for a thousand years. (Revelation 20:4 ISR)

Furthermore, these saints, these set-apart ones, get to avoid a fate far worse than any Tribulation trial or death (Revelation 12:11). The fate that they avoid is the one that is reserved for all who loved their own lives so much that they gave in to the mark of the beast and worshipped his image in order to be able to buy, sell, and trade. Look at the following verses:

> And I heard a loud voice from the Dwelling Place saying to the seven messengers, "Go and pour out the bowls of the wrath of Elohim on the earth." And the first went and poured out his bowl upon the earth, and an evil and wicked sore came upon the men, those having the mark of the beast and those worshipping his image. (Revelation 16:1-:2 ISR)

There are six more bowls of curses that I will not quote their entire verses here, but you can continue to read about them in your copy of the Word in Revelation 16. I will say, though, that these curses include the death of the creatures in the sea, being given blood to drink, being burned by the sun, pain that causes you to gnaw your tongue, drought, demonic possession of the rulers of the entire world, a great earthquake, and huge hailstones falling on men.

Let's pick back up at Revelation 13 verse 16-18 now:

> And he causes all, both small and great, and rich and poor, and free and slave, to be given a mark upon their right hand or upon their foreheads, and that no one should be able to buy or sell except he that has the mark or the name of the beast, or the number of his name. Here is the wisdom! He who has understanding, let him calculate the number of the beast, for it is the number of a man, and his number is six hundred and sixty six. (Revelation 13:16-18 ISR)

Think about what I am about to say very carefully. When you know that refusing to take the mark could mean sudden death, yet you would be gaining the blessing and honor of ruling and reigning with Yahuweh and His Son forever as well as not having to experience the terrible tortures and curses reserved for those who do take the mark, there is no comparison. And there are even more places in Revelation that tell of additional tortures you will receive before your final torture, called the second death, which never ends day or night in the lake of fire. This is where the false prophet, the beast, and the dragon (Satan) will spend eternity as well.

The following verse shows the forever torture and torment reserved for those giving in to the beast and its image. Taking the mark is not worth it to be able to temporarily stay alive. You've heard the saying "a fate worse than death"? Well, this is it!

> And the smoke of their torture goes up forever and ever. And they have no rest day or night, those worshipping the beast and his image, also if anyone receives the mark of his name. (Revelation 14:11 ISR)

When looking at all the world-changing events that have rapidly taken place in 2020, especially with the introduction of the Covid-19 virus, we need to be prepared to make the decisions that may be demanded of us, soon! Whose side will we be on? If we believe the theory of a pre-tribulation rapture, we will not prepare our hearts and minds to do the battle needed to take a stand for being able to refuse the mark of the beast. We will not be as diligent to hide His Word in our hearts so that we do not sin against our Creator. I am grateful for the Scriptures that show me the truth of how to stand and be truly on the winning side and to not believe in a rapture theory. And my prayer is that you know these things as well.

CHAPTER 13

*What if you found out the way to recognize
the anti-messiah is to know the Law?*

WE HAVE JUST FINISHED OUR discussion concerning the common belief of a rapture before the Tribulation. Now I want to focus on how not to be fooled by the anti-messiah during the Tribulation. Yahushua's first words when asked by His disciples about the times to come were:

> "...Take heed that no one deceives you." (Matthew 24:4 NKJV)

Then Yahushua began to describe what must take place before He returns to gather His people. I won't quote all of Matthew 24 here but will point out some key verses concerning the anti-messiah and being deceived or fooled:

> And many false prophets shall rise up and lead many astray. And because of the increase in lawlessness, the love of many shall become cold. (Matthew 24:11-12 ISR)

> For false messiahs and false prophets shall arise, and they shall show great signs and wonders, so as to lead

astray, if possible, even the chosen ones. (Matthew 24:24 ISR)

And the apostle John warns us as well:

Little children, it is the last hour. And as you have heard that the anti-messiah is coming, even now many anti-messiahs have come. This is how we know that it is the last hour. (1 John 2:18 ISR)

In the verses below, notice the warning given by Paul, Silas, and Timothy to the believers in Thessalonica:

[3] Let no one deceive you in any way, because the falling away is to come first, and the man of lawlessness is to be revealed, the son of destruction, [4] who opposes and exalts himself above all that is called Elohim or that is worshipped, so that he sits as Elohim in the Dwelling Place of Elohim, showing himself that he is Elohim. [5] Do you not remember that I told you this while I was still with you? [6] And now you know what restrains, for him to be revealed in his time. [7] For the secret of lawlessness is already at work—only until he who now restrains comes out of the midst. [8] And then the lawless one shall be revealed, whom the Master shall consume with the Spirit of His mouth and bring to naught with the manifestation of His coming. [9] The coming of the *lawless one* is according to the working of Satan, with all power and signs and wonder of falsehood, [10] and with all deceit of unrighteousness in those perishing, because they did not receive the love of the truth, in order for them to be saved. [11] And for this reason Elohim sends them a working of delusion, for them to believe the falsehood, [12] in order that all should be judged who

did not believe the truth, but have delighted in the unrighteousness. (2 Thessalonians 2:3-12 ISR)

When I read verses 10 and 12 above, I notice these words: "did not receive the love of the truth," "did not believe the truth," and "have delighted in unrighteousness." The people who receive delusion are the ones who do not love Yahuweh's truth. So, what is this truth? Let's let scripture define scripture:

Your righteousness *is* an everlasting righteousness, and your law *is* truth. (Psalm 119:142 NKJV)

You are near, O יהוה, and all Your commands are truth. (Psalm 119:151 ISR)

According to Thayer's Greek Lexicon, "unrighteousness" in the Thessalonian verses above is defined as *unrighteousness of heart and life*. Unrighteousness of heart is lack of faith. And unrighteousness of life is our lack of works of obedience to His commands in our life. And if we are familiar and comfortable not knowing and following our Maker's laws, then it is safe to say that we will be familiar and comfortable with lawlessness. And if we are comfortable with lawlessness, we *will* be deceived by the lawless one. How many places in the above quoted passage in Thessalonians does it mention these words "lawlessness," "lawless one," and "unrighteousness"?

Again, I think of the book of James where Scripture states we must have *both* belief and works (faith and obedience). They go hand in hand. I've written about this several times. Unrighteousness is the opposite of right living and right thinking, which come from the heart. So if I do not have the love of the truth, I will act in unrighteousness, and then I will be deceived.

Look at Titus 1:16 ISR, "They profess to know Elohim, but in works they deny Him, being abominable, and disobedient, and unfit for any good work."

If we want to be able to recognize the anti-messiah and not

be deceived into taking his mark, we have to have a love for the truth of our Maker, which is to believe in His Son and obey His commands. This is as simple as I can put it. Look at who the prophecy tells will be able to resist taking the mark:

> And I saw thrones—and they sat on them, and judgment was given to them—and the lives of those who had been beheaded because of the witness they bore to יהושע and because of the Word of Elohim, and who did not worship the beast, nor his image, and did not receive his mark upon their foreheads or upon their hands. And they lived and reigned with Messiah for a thousand years. (Revelation 20:4 ISR)

"…because of the witness they bore to יהושע and because of the Word of Elohim…"—these words are also recorded *together* over and over again in one form or another in Revelation 1:2,9; 6:9; 12:11,7; 2 Timothy 3:15; and 1 Peter 1:2, showing that we need to have both the Word of Elohim (which is the Torah and the Truth) along with the witness of the Messiah (which is our faith in Him) in order to overcome! They knew the Messiah and obeyed the Word of Elohim. It takes both. Again, they are inseparable. And this is exactly the opposite of what Satan wants us to believe! You see, our enemy's job is to sever the Word of Elohim from the witness of the Messiah so we cannot recognize the counterfeit messiah.

> Here is the endurance of the set-apart ones, here are those guarding the commands of Elohim and the belief of יהושע. (Revelation 14:12 ISR)

These saints, these set-apart ones endured and never gave in to worshiping the beast or taking his mark. Sure, they were beheaded, but their reward is far greater for their martyrdom than the fate that awaits those who took the mark and stayed alive a little longer. As we discussed in the previous chapter, those taking the mark suffer tremendous torture on earth during the Tribulation as well as for all eternity in the lake of fire. These truths are strong enough deterrents for me that I never want to forget:

> And the smoke of their torment goes up forever and ever, and they have no rest, day or night, these worshippers of the beast and its image, and whoever receives the mark of its name. (Revelation 14:11 ESV)

So what else does Scripture tell us about how to recognize the anti-messiah?

> He will speak against the Most High and wear down the saints of the Highest One, and he will intend to make alterations in times and in law; and they will be handed over to him for a time, times, and half a time. (Daniel 7:25 NASB)

Look at several other translations of this particular verse in order to understand exactly what he will seek to change:

> NIV "...and try to change the set times and the laws..."

> NLT "...will try to change their sacred festivals and laws..."

> KJV "...and think to change times and laws..."

> Darby Bible Translation "...and think to change seasons and the law..."

> ISR "...and it intends to change appointed times and law..."

Remember, as we discussed in the beginning chapters, that the above references to "seasons," "times," or "sacred festivals" are Yahuweh's moedim, His appointed times, which are His weekly Sabbath days and His seven annual feast days as outlined in Leviticus 23:1-4.

The anti-messiah will not uphold these appointed times. He is against them and as noted above, he will seek to change them and has already begun to do so to the appointed time of Yahuweh's weekly Sabbath. As I discussed in the earlier chapter entitled "What if you found out the Sabbath was never changed from the seventh day?", our Creator never changed His Sabbath day from the seventh day to the first day of the week. But there is an institution that claims the authority to do so—the Roman Catholic Institution. You can learn more about their claim here: **https://romeschallenge.com/**

We are so grateful we found out about these appointed times and how to keep and guard them. Their significance not only points us to the prophecies of our Savior but will help us recognize the anti-messiah and his mark. Remember my discussion of a "sign" being a "mark" in Hebrew and of the verses where our Father says that His Sabbaths are a sign between Him and His people forever? Here are two links to show "sign" meaning "mark":

https://www.bing.com/translator?ref=TThis&&text=a%20 sign%20is%20a%20mark&from=&to=he

https://biblehub.com/hebrew/226.htm

(Be sure to scroll down to *Strong's Exhaustive Concordance* on the second link.)

To be *marked* or *sealed* by our Heavenly Father as being "His" is another very good reason to be obedient to our Heavenly Father's commands, especially concerning His seventh-day Sabbath and His feast days. We have become determined to do our best to guard these appointed times and gather with others during them.

And in further discussing Daniel 7:25 above, I want us to note that the prophet Daniel was speaking of a future time when the anti-messiah would still be seeking to change the appointed times and the Law, during the Tribulation years. This time frame proves the seventh-day Sabbath and laws to keep the Feast days never went away and continue to be commands that our Heavenly Father wants all of His people to keep even into the end times. The following scriptures show that the Sabbath remains: Matthew 24:20, Hebrews 4:3-11, and Isaiah 66:23.

Could our Heavenly Father be preparing us for such a time as the Tribulation, protecting us from deceit, by picking this moment in history to reveal and return His people to keeping (guarding) His Sabbaths? I know something significant is happening in the faith community. And so often we have found, as we meet more and more people (who are beginning to love and obey Yahuweh with all their heart, especially in learning to keep His Sabbaths), that the common report of each of us is that we all thought (at the beginning of our own personal journeys) we were the only ones seeing these truths. This tells me this is not a movement orchestrated by man, but is a movement of the Set-apart Spirit of Truth, of Yahuweh Himself, calling His people back to Him in set-apartness, as He predicted in His Word through His prophets.

> O יהוה, my strength and my stronghold and my refuge, in the day of distress the nations shall come to You from the ends of the earth and say, 'Our fathers have inherited only falsehood, futility, and there is no value in them.' Would a man make mighty ones for himself, which are not mighty ones? 'Therefore see, I am causing them to know, this time I cause them to

know My hand and My might. And they shall know that My Name is יהוה !' (Jeremiah 16:19-21 ISR)

If we do find ourselves living during the days of the Great Tribulation, when there will be extreme pressure for everyone to accept the mark of the beast, how will we be able to resist, especially if we cannot lay down our lives *now* for His sake and take a stand for obeying His commands?

I pray I will have this kind of strength to endure, should I live to see the time of this prophecy. The words "to stand" and "endure" have always sparked a desire in me to be able to identify with those set-apart ones! And the people who know and keep the Sabbaths and the Feast days will be the ones who will recognize the anti-messiah for who he is. Because they know the Law, they will recognize exactly what he is seeking to change in the Father's set-apart times and will know the difference between the real and the counterfeit. They will not be deceived.

CHAPTER 14

*What if you found out our Heavenly Father
does not hear the prayers of sinners?*

I 'M SURE YOU'RE THINKING, *WHAT is she talking about?
Does she not believe in the sinner's prayer?* But take a deep
breath and then look at what Yahuweh's Word says. Let's
look at several translations for two different verses to better understand exactly what is being said:

Psalm 66:18:

> If I regard iniquity in my heart, the Lord will not hear
> *me.* (KJV)

> If I regard wickedness in my heart, the Lord will not
> hear. (NASB)

> If I had cherished sin in my heart, the Lord would not
> have listened. (NIV)

> If I have seen wickedness in my heart; יהוה would
> not hear. (ISR)

John 9:31:

> Now we know that God heareth not sinners; but if
> any man be a worshipper of God, and doeth His will,
> him He heareth. (KJV)

We know that God does not listen to sinners; but if someone is God-fearing and does His will, He listens to him. (NASB)

We know that God does not listen to sinners. He listens to the godly person who does his will. (NIV)

And we know that Elohim does not hear sinners. But if anyone fears Elohim and does His desire, He hears him. (ISR)

When I read these verses, I knew I didn't fully understand them. I wondered what I was missing. Then my next question was, "Are there other verses in His Word that will help me understand these verses?"

Again using Biblehub.com, the very useful online tool that displays several translations of any given verse on a single page and cross-references verses, I found that Psalm 66:18 is cross-referenced with John 9:31 (the above two quoted verses) as well as cross-referenced with James 4:3, Deuteronomy 1:45, and passages in Job, Psalms, Proverbs, and Isaiah as well. Look at our Father's reaction to the prideful actions of the Israelites in Deuteronomy:

"So I spoke to you, but you would not listen and rebelled against the mouth of יהוה, and acted proudly, and went up into the mountain. Then the Amorites who dwelt in that mountain came out against you and chased you as bees do, and drove you back from Se'ir to Hormah. And you returned and wept before יהוה, but יהוה would not listen to your voice nor give ear to you. (Deuteronomy 1:43-45 ISR)

I never knew there were verses that showed that my Heavenly Father does not acknowledge, even when weeping and crying are involved. This is not what I was taught. What I had always heard and believed was that My Father always listens. He is "all knowing," and I had always assumed He hears all prayers. Now I'm reading that His listening and hearing are conditional.

How can that be?

My Father has conditions for even hearing prayers?

I will quote a few more of the cross-referenced verses I found. Notice the spiritual condition of those He refuses to acknowledge:

יהוה *is* far from the wrong ones, But He hears the prayer of the righteous. (Proverbs 15:29 ISR)

Let them then call on me, but I answer not; Let them seek me, but not find me. Because they hated knowledge and did not choose the fear of יהוה (Proverbs 1:28-29 ISR)

After reading all these verses, it was beginning to make sense to me. If we don't have the humble fear (respect) and love of our Heavenly Father enough to listen to Him and follow His instructions, why should He listen to and answer us?

He knows the motives and the condition of our hearts—whether we are truly repentant or whether we are still holding onto pride to stubbornly live our own way. Now notice what He says for us to do in order for Him to hear us:

If My people who are called by My name will humble themselves, and pray and seek My face, and turn from their wicked ways, then I will hear from heaven, and will forgive their sin and heal their land. (2 Chronicles 7:14 NKJV)

Many of you know this commonly quoted Scripture. Notice this passage begins with the word "if." Do you see that our Heavenly Father's ear and blessings are contingent upon several actions on our part *before* He hears and heals? He requires humility, prayer, seeking His face, and turning away from our own ways for Him to then hear, forgive, and to heal.

As I began to write this chapter about having our prayers heard, I had no idea the next point was going to be a part of it. When I write, it surprises me what verses and subjects come up in my spirit. And I almost didn't include the next discussion, as I knew it to be controversial today, even within the Christian community. But this is a subject very near and dear to my heart. And after I wrote the following thoughts, I could see that this is only *one* example among many paths and patterns of human behavior where we go astray in defending ourselves and our self-determining walks of pride that keeps our Maker from hearing us. These human behaviors (choices) end up being against our Heavenly Father's will for how He created every human being to live and to love. It helps to keep in mind the basic truth that our Heavenly Father's righteousness does not change, neither before nor after He sent His Son. His definitions of sin and righteousness never change. So here goes…

I used to be very proud of being able to say I had gay friends in high school, and even later in my adult years. Now I know this is something I should never have been proud of. I wasn't thinking or caring about their relationship with their Heavenly Father. I was only thinking about how "tolerant," "liberal," and "nonjudgmental" I looked and could claim to be by being proud of their lifestyle choices and that I was their friend. I didn't love them the way that the Creator designed for me to love—and that was wrong! In looking back, I can now say I was selfish and even hated my gay friends.

What? Hated?

Yes, I said "hated." And not in the sense that we understand this word "hate" in English today. In Greek, the word "hate" often means to "love less." And as I revealed in an earlier chapter, in Hebrew the word "hate" not only can mean "to detest" but also can mean "unloved"; and *I did not detest my gay friends at all.* I simply loved them less than I loved the fact that I could be tolerant and nonjudgmental. Do you see that my love and concern was not focused on them, but rather on me and how I looked to them and to the world? I was *so* proud of being "tolerant" of their lifestyle. I even lost one of my kindest friends, who died of AIDS. I was still under the deception in my pride of calling him my friend because of his choice to be gay. Do you see how wrong I was? I knew what my Heavenly Father and His Son said in the Scriptures and still cared more about myself than I did about his eternal relationship with his Maker and His Son.

Satan is a liar and is the best at twisting the truth to tickle our ears and to make us proud of decisions that harm us and our relationship with our Maker. Our enemy deceives us into acting on our feelings and desires rather than on the Word of our Creator. He cunningly gets us to believe twisted conclusions like these:

> *It's not wrong to live the way that I feel is right. The Father is so merciful and loving He wouldn't condemn me for what I do and the way I am or the way I choose to live. He made me and loves me. His Son died so I can be free.*

But free from what? Yahushua died to free us from the bondage of sin, not from our responsibility to obey His commands. Do you see the problem of stopping short of the whole truth? We cannot realistically say that He loves us so much that we can then declare our own ways are "good." It doesn't work that way. His love never excuses us to willfully sin against Him and His Law. Satan lies and robs us; it's his job. And when we decide to justify our own feelings and desires, we believe his lies and bow down to him and his kingdom even if we think we're not.

If we are honest about it, we will admit that we have all chosen paths at one time or another that harm us. Yet our Maker loves us so much that He gives us the power and the incentive not to stay there but to overcome. Remember, "evil" in His eyes is anything that goes against His truth and His will. He says *overcome evil with good* and do not be deceived into calling evil "good." He knows we have inherited lies, taken wrong paths, embraced curses, yet He warns us that if we deliberately continue in these paths, it will destroy us and our relationship with Him in the end. And this is why He cannot listen to (heed) our requests when we are in this deliberate and defiant state. Look at this next scripture:

> But they refused to listen, and they shrugged their shoulders, and stopped their ears from hearing. And they made their hearts like flint against hearing the Torah, and the words, which יהוה of hosts had sent by His Spirit through the former prophets. Therefore great wrath came from יהוה of hosts. And it came to be: as He called and they did not hear, so let them call, but I shall not hear, said יהוה of hosts. (Zechariah 7:11-13 ISR)

The next verse says by siding with the popular ways of this world and its present but temporary ruler, we actually become an enemy of our Maker.

> Adulterers and adulteresses! Do you not know that friendship with the world is enmity with Elohim? Whoever therefore wants to be a friend of the world makes himself an enemy of Elohim. (James 4:4 ISR)

We can only serve one of two masters, and to be friends with the world makes us the enemy of our Heavenly Father, and that scares me! We are either on our way to becoming children of light or children of darkness—a choice made by our actions.

Knowing all of this, how can we keep silent if we really care about someone? What is the proverb that talks about the sting of a friend?

> Faithful are the wounds of a friend, but deceitful are
> the kisses of an enemy. (Proverbs 27:6 NASB)

Am I only to speak what others I care deeply about want to hear? Is this having true love for them? Or is it, in fact, "hate" (to love them less)? I am so done with thinking and believing that way. I will speak the truth to them in love!

And are we not even going to warn our neighbor simply because we fear being labeled "intolerant," "bigoted," or "judgmental"?

> Watch yourselves. If your brother sins, rebuke him;
> and if he repents, forgive him. (Luke 17:3 Berean
> Study Bible)

> You shall not hate your fellow countryman in your
> heart; you may certainly rebuke your neighbor, but
> you are not to incur sin because of him. Leviticus
> 19:17 NASB)

If we truly care, we will let the Set-apart Spirit guide us, giving us the right words and the right timing, to warn our neighbor. And I have learned now to care about and love my friends and family in the way my Heavenly Father says to love. I care deeply about their relationship with their Maker because I know the truth, and no longer have my eyes on me but on their freedom, peace, protection, and eternity. I try my best to be patient and speak the truth in love and in the Father's timing. It is wrong of me to selfishly shy away from trying to share what we are commanded to share simply because it is easier not to or I am afraid of being labeled "judgmental" and/or "intolerant." Paul obviously cared about the new believers in Ephesus, as he spoke clearly and truthfully to them:

> And you were dead in trespasses and sins, in which
> you once walked according to the course of this
> world, according to the ruler of the authority of the

air, of the spirit that is now working in the sons of disobedience, among whom also we all once lived in the lusts of our flesh, doing the desires of the flesh and of the mind, and were by nature children of wrath, as also the rest. (Ephesians 2:1-3 ISR).

I know today that these words are not popular and many refuse to hear and will disagree with what I'm saying, but please don't give me the credit for defining homosexuality or any other behavior as "sin" (lawlessness). I didn't write the Book! Nor did I create life or design the way it should be lived, nor the consequences for ignoring it. So if my caring enough to speak my Father's truth gets me in trouble with those caught up in the "world," then so be it.

Leviticus 18 is a chapter in His Law listing His commands in which we are not to defile ourselves that I previously touched on concerning sexual relations between parents and their children and grandchildren all the way to sexual relations with aunts and neighbor's wives as well as having intercourse between men, between women, and between humans and beasts. All of these are abominable to our Creator.

While reading the below verses, notice how our lack of the love and respect due to our Creator leads to more sins:

> For since the creation of the world His invisible *qualities* have been clearly seen, being understood from what has been made, both His everlasting power and Mightiness, for them to be without excuse, because, although they knew Elohim, they did not esteem Him as Elohim, nor gave thanks, but became vain in their reasonings, and their undiscerning heart was darkened. Claiming to be wise, they became fools, and changed the esteem of the incorruptible Elohim into the likeness of an image of corruptible man, and of birds and of four-

26

footed beasts and of reptiles. Therefore Elohim gave them up to uncleanness in the lust of their hearts, to disrespect their bodies among themselves, who changed the truth of Elohim into the falsehood, and worshipped and served what was created rather than the Creator, who is blessed forever. Amen. Because of this Elohim gave them over to degrading passions. For even their women exchanged natural relations for what is against nature, and likewise, the men also, having left natural relations with woman, burned in their lust for one another, men with men committing indecency, and receiving back the reward which was due for their straying. And even as they did not think it worthwhile to possess the knowledge of Elohim, Elohim gave them over to a worthless mind, to do what is improper, having been filled with all unrighteousness, whoring, wickedness, greed, evil; filled with envy, murder, fighting, deceit, evil habits, whisperers, slanderers, haters of Elohim, insolent, proud, boasters, devisers of evils, disobedient to parents, without discernment, covenant breakers, unloving, unforgiving, ruthless; who, though they know the righteousness of Elohim, that those who practice such deserve death, not only do the same but also approve of those who practice them. (Romans 1:20-32 ISR)

Therefore, O man, you are without excuse. (Romans 2:1a ISR)

Or do you despise the riches of His kindness, and tolerance, and patience, not knowing that the kindness of Elohim leads you to repentance? But according to your hardness and your unrepentant heart you are treasuring up for yourself wrath in the day of wrath and revelation of the righteous judgment of Elohim, who "shall render to each one according to his works" everlasting life to those who by persistence in good work seek for esteem, and respect, and incorruptibility; but wrath and displeasure to those who are self-seeking and do not obey the truth, but obey unrighteousness... (Romans 2:4-8 ISR)

I had always thought that all idolatry amounted to was the worshipping of images and statues, but now I know that idolatry is lusting after anything that we love and honor more than our Creator. When we do not esteem Him for Who He is but give that esteem elsewhere, to ourselves, to others and what our own hands have accomplished, it is idolatry just like King Nebuchadnezzar did as recorded in Daniel 4:30 (the story of a king worth reading about in Daniel chapters 3-4). And I believe I have shared what Paul's letter says to the Colossians below which is very eye opening in defining idolatry.

Therefore put to death your members which are on the earth: whoring, uncleanness, passion, evil desire and greed of gain, which is idolatry.(Colossians 3:5-6 ISR)

It is helpful to look at this verse in other translations as well at:
http://www.biblehub.com/colossians/3-5.htm. Paul also warns about lust and idolatry in 1 Corinthians 10:6-14.

How can any of us stay in the popular ways of this world and still try to claim the promises of our Maker that is reserved for those who love and obey Him? We have been so blind.

It's so easy to lose our perspective and excuse our behavior, because we're human. And our enemy will do anything to turn our head and our heart away from the truth and keep us from our blessings and our future of being with our Heavenly Father and

His Son forever. As you look around us, you will see the trends in sexuality he is using to distract today. Always remember, we were never designed to lead the way.

> Oh יהוה, I know the way of man is not in himself,
> it is not for man who walks to direct his own steps.
> (Jeremiah 10:23 ISR)

We either want what He wants for our lives or we don't, and we are willing to do what it takes to get it or we're not. It really is black and white—not fifty shades of gray. His Son said we are either for Him or we are against Him (Matthew 12:30). We must be willing to lay down our lives, to overcome our own desires, for His sake as well as for our own. Our forever destiny depends on it.

Be careful not to fall into Satan's trap of excusing ourselves by concluding that we cannot change and should not even try to overcome the things we were born with. We are all born under sin and with a tendency to sin. Think about it: If I am born with certain tendencies that are against my Creator's will, and I assume that I can't change or overcome them, then there goes my free will; I no longer have a choice. This is a wrong conclusion again, where Satan begins with a truth and then twists it. We *can* overcome our tendencies, our inherited curses, our desires of the flesh, our confusion, our rebellion, our pride, our past, and the lies we have inherited and learned!

If we say we cannot overcome sin, then this belief makes a mockery of the verses that say we *can* be cleansed of all unrighteousness, that we *can* walk in newness of life, just like our Messiah did in righteousness.

> He gave his life to free us from every kind of sin,
> to cleanse us, and to make us his very own people,
> totally committed to doing good deeds. (Titus 2:14
> NLT)

Listen to the words that John says over and over again about being cleansed and not sinning.

> If we say that we have fellowship with Him, and walk in darkness, we lie and are not doing the truth. But if we walk in the light as He is in the light, we have fellowship with one another, and the blood of יהושע Messiah His Son cleanses us from all sin. If we say that we have no sin, we are misleading ourselves, and the truth is not in us. If we confess our sins, He is trustworthy and righteous to forgive us the sins and cleanse us from all unrighteousness. If we say that we have not sinned, we make Him a liar, and His Word is not in us. (1 John 1:6-10 ISR)

Our Maker wants us to be real.

> My little children, I write this to you, so that you do not sin. And if anyone sins, we have an Intercessor with the Father, יהושע Messiah, a righteous One. And He Himself is an atoning offering for our sins, and not for ours only but also for all the world. And by this we know that we know Him, if we guard His commands. The one who says, "I know Him," and does not guard His commands, is a liar, and the truth is not in him. But whoever guards His Word, truly the love of Elohim has been perfected in him. By this we know that we are in Him. The one who says he stays in Him ought himself also to walk, even as He walked. (1 John 2:1-6 ISR)

I know I quoted a lot of verses, but John is very clear here. and his words are stark. For us to deny that the Spirit has the power to be able to change us into righteous children to serve a righteous Creator is blasphemy and is unpardonable! Why do we not use this power of the Spirit to overcome what we let into our lives as well as what we have inherited (the generational curses we were born with)? Is it because we like what we like more than we like what our Maker likes? He really *is* asking us to lay down our lives for His sake. When we pridefully defend the behaviors that we like, but know down deep inside are against our Creator, we are giving in to Satan's desire.

And when deception takes over, none of us can discern the difference between our Father's desires and our own desires. We begin to call our own will "His."

By staying in the world and its ways, we are growing accustomed to calling the wrong actions that we have chosen "good," while we encourage others to do the same. We are getting to the point even in our churches that we can't tell the difference anymore.

> Do not love the world nor that which is in the world. If anyone loves the world, the love of the Father is not in him. Because all that is in the world—the lust of the flesh, the lust of the eyes, and the pride of life –is not of the Father but is of the world. And the world passes away, and the lust of it, but the one doing the desire of Elohim remains forever. (1 John 2:15-17 ISR)

Bottom line: we were created in His image to be able to learn and know the difference between right and wrong according to His will, His definition of what sin is and what righteousness is, *not* according to the world's definition. We have no right to change Yahuweh's definitions. Our Creator's character and instructions for how He wants us to live and to love does not change. We must take into consideration more than a few verses as we determine how to live our lives, and we must test, for ourselves, what others around us are saying by looking in His word. We owe it to ourselves and to our Maker.

Too many people assume when they identify themselves as

being a Christian, that they are followers of Messiah. But how can this be when we really don't follow in His footsteps, walking as He walked, obeying His Father's commands? He humbly walked in His Father's Laws! We don't do that, especially when we say the Law was abolished. And we even twist the commands we do agree with to satisfy our own desires.

Our Messiah overcame every sin He was tempted to give in to. We must do the same through the power of the Spirit, not denying His leadership in the commands of Yahuweh. Yahushua never broke any of His Father's Laws, or He couldn't have been the perfect (sinless) Lamb. He fought Satan off in the wilderness by combating the enemy's twisted use of Yahuweh's Word. Our enemy knows Scripture too! Yahushua fought back with His Father's words—the wisdom of the Torah of old—with the full weight of their unadulterated and intended meaning and power. This is how we, too, must fight, against the lies we have inherited and against our own evil desires, by knowing and following the Torah, the Word of our Heavenly Father.

His Spirit never goes against His Word and has the power to raise a life from the dead. How can we deny having the ability to be raised from a state of *walking dead* in our sins, to a state of *walking in newness of life*?

Remember that His Word is sharper than any two-edge sword that slices between truth and lies. Our enemy, for sure, does not want us to look at it, know it, follow it, or wield it for battle! So, he lies to us. If he can't convince us that the long--awaited Messiah hasn't come to Earth, then he attempts to twist our understanding of *why* He came, to make us believe the Messiah came to abolish His Father's Law as we discussed in Chapter 7 of this book. This wrong belief opens the door to every kind of twisted interpretation of our Messiah's and the apostles' words in the New Testament so that we justify our fleshly desires and actions. Of course, our deceit seems correct when we only look to a small handful of verses for living our lives. We have to look at the whole Word. The words in the New Testament support the laws in the Old Testament. It all goes together.

Remember 1 John 2:4 says we are liars if we claim to know Him yet do not guard His commands. We are responsible for what we know! And if we didn't know these things, then as soon as they have been revealed, we are responsible. We are no longer to walk in the deceit of our hearts.

But you may ask, "How am I supposed to just all of a sudden stop walking the way I have been used to walking?" Remember the parable of the prodigal son? Our Father is right there waiting for us to take that first humble step back home to Him. He loves us so much and has so many good things He wants to give us. But it is up to us to turn around and come back from all the waste places we have been.

At the very second that we stop and humbly ask for His help, in that very nanosecond, we are no longer a sinner in our Father's eyes. He sees our repentant heart. Our pride is gone. He knows when we are turning back to Him, and He is right there waiting to hear and to answer before we even begin to ask for His forgiveness in His Son's Name. This humbleness is what He's waiting for.

> And it shall be that before they call, I answer. And while they are still speaking, I hear. (Isaiah 66:24 ISR)

I want my Maker to hear me, and I am sure you do too!

> The eyes of יהוה are on the righteous, and His ears unto their cry. (Psalm 34:15 ISR)

There is nothing too hard for Him.

CHAPTER 15

*Now that I know about His appointed times,
how do I go about honoring them?*

L ET ME START WITH THE basics that I learned:
Our Maker's set-apart times are everlasting. These
appointed times are appointments with our Creator and
His people. It is well worth learning about these laws and obeying them to the best of our ability. Every year He reveals something new! Our learning is never stagnant or boring, but exciting
as we find out more and more of His awesome design for how
He wants us to live and to love Him and each other.

A complete list of these set-apart times is found in Leviticus
23 as well as throughout Scripture. We've already discussed that
they were put in motion from the beginning:

> And Elohim said, "Let lights come to be in the
> expanse of the heavens to separate the day from the
> night, and let them be for signs and appointed times,
> and for days and years..." (Genesis 1:14 ISR)

What were these lights?

> And Elohim made two great lights; the greater light
> to rule the day, and the lesser light to rule the night,
> and the stars. (Genesis 1:16 ISR)

His lights—the sun, moon, and stars—determine these appointed times, also called "seasons" in other translations. KJV also calls these commanded set-apart gatherings "holy convocations." His desire and command for us to observe these times never went away. They are His *mo'edim*, which is plural for *mo'ed* in Hebrew. They include all His Sabbaths from the seventh-day Sabbath to each appointed Feast listed below. And notice in Leviticus 1:1 that our Maker also says we are to declare these times as set-apart gatherings. These are the gathering times that I believe the writer of Hebrews tells us to not forsake in the "gathering together of the saints." I have included below in parenthesis the ISR translation for listing the appointed times of Leviticus chapter 23:

- Passover (Pesah in Hebrew)
- Feast of Unleavened Bread (Festival of Matzot)
- Feast of Weeks (Shavuot, also known as Pentecost)
- Feast of Trumpets ("a remembrance of Teru'ah," or blowing of trumpets)
- Day of Atonement (Yom haKippurim)
- Feast of Tabernacles (Festival of Sukkot)

There is a seventh appointed time called the "Wave Sheaf Offering" or "First Fruits Offering," found in Leviticus 23:10-15. This particular date connects the Feast of Unleavened Bread with Shavuot. In the following paragraphs I will tell you how we learned to count the days from the Wave Sheaf Offering to the day of Shavuot

And יהוה spoke to Mosheh, saying, 'Speak to the children of Yisra'el, and say to them, "The appointed times of יהוה, which you are to proclaim as set-apart gatherings, My appointed times, are these: six days work is done, but the seventh day is a Sabbath of rest, a set-apart gathering. You do no work; it is a Sabbath to יהוה in all your dwellings. (Leviticus 23:1-3 ISR)

As I stated in previous chapters that at the beginning of our discoveries of the lies we had inherited, and then as we learned about our Heavenly Father's Sabbath, we thought we were the only ones, especially in our community, who were being shown these truths. Although the majority of churches still do not keep the Sabbath, the appointed times (feast days), or believe in obeying the Torah, it is encouraging to see and hear of a growing number of congregations, including those that gather in homes, that have begun to see these truths and to obey them. Remember Scott Hillman's YouTube video I introduced you to in chapter two? It was entitled "AoG Pastor Changes to Sabbath and Feast Observance. Why?" It has become very encouraging for us to find out about him and other denominational pastors waking up to our Father's everlasting commands. We continue to pray for our own local pastors and their congregations to do the same. Many of them are our friends and family.

It was about nine years ago, when we were first waking up to more of our Father's truths, that we found others to gather with (Hebrews 10:25) who were being shown the same things we were discovering. We were shocked at how many people even in our small town and surrounding area were learning to walk this walk. And we were additionally blessed recently with several new friends who have been learning to obey Yahuweh's Word, as well.

Although we may not agree on every detail of how to determine the dates of the feast days nor on exactly how we call on the name of our Father and His Son, we can see others' newfound love for our Creator's commands and for learning His ways, especially in keeping His seventh-day Sabbath and removing the pagan traditions from their lives as we have. We are all learning in our pursuit to walk as our Messiah walked in His Father's ways (1 John 2:3-6).

So, with the leadership of the Set-apart Spirit of Truth, and being armed with His Word, we carefully investigated what other like-minded followers were sharing on the internet, as well as asked about the practices of the followers we met in person.

One year Kevin and I realized we had been overlooking something in Genesis concerning the sun that our Father uses to determine His appointed times. And just before Passover, as we were reading Genesis 1:14 connecting the sun's cycle to the determining of Yahuweh's year and seasons, a good friend of ours gave me the number of his friend Peggy that he had gathered with on several Shabbats (Hebrew for "Sabbaths"). I called her, and we quickly connected in many areas of our walk. Yahuweh is so wonderful and knows just what we need in His timing! She and her son had been determining the timing of the Passover in the manner that Kevin and I had just begun to investigate. Really pouring over Genesis now with fresh eyes, I remembered how Yahuweh tells us the end from the beginning (Isaiah 46:10). Doesn't the word "genesis" mean origin, source, root, beginning, start? I had no idea, for most of my life as a believer, that the book of Genesis was so important and was to be such a part of our lives!

So this spring Kevin, Mother, and I discovered how to include the fact that not only does the moon measure the beginning of each month, but the *sun* measures the beginning of each *year.* Yahuweh begins His year in the spring, as this verse tells us:

> This month *shall be* your beginning of months; it *shall be* the first month of the year to you. (Exodus 12:2 NKJV)

Yahuweh said this to the ancient Israelites (Hebrew people) just before He led them out of Egypt, as He was giving instructions that included killing the Passover lamb and placing the blood on the doorpost. Read Exodus 12:1-11. Also note the result of the seventh plague and what time of year it was when the hail struck the barley and the flax.

> And the flax and the barley were struck, for the barley was in the head and the flax was in bud. But the wheat and the spelt were not struck, for they were late crops. (Exodus 9:31-32 ISR)

It was springtime.

It takes a year, approximately 365.256 days, for the Earth to complete its orbit around the sun. *Scientific American* online has an article dated March 20, 2013, concerning the vernal equinox that states: "Although popularly described as 'the first day of spring' in the northern hemisphere, the annual event is actually much more important than that. More than any other event, it marks the beginning of the astronomical year."

I was amazed at how *Scientific America* confirmed this Biblical yearly event, the vernal equinox, as the beginning of the astronomical year, which also determines, along with the cycle of the moon, the beginning of Yahuweh's new year.

The definition of the vernal equinox is when daytime and nighttime are of approximately equal duration. The website earthsky.org has an excellent and simple article: **http://earthsky.org/astronomy-essentials/everything-you-need-to-know-vernal-or-spring-equinox.** From a scientific standpoint, this article states: "The equinox is an event that happens on our sky's dome and is a seasonal marker of Earth's orbit around the sun." I like how this writer uses the word "seasonal," because several translations use the word "seasons" in the verse below:

> ..."Let there be lights in the expanse of the heavens to separate the day from the night. And let them be for signs and for seasons, and for days and years," (Genesis 1:14 ESV)

I had always thought that the word "seasons" meant fall, winter, spring, and summer, but now in looking at the Hebrew origin and meaning of this word, I found it means "*moed*" in Hebrew, Strong's 4150, for appointed times that are our Father's feast days. The pieces were beginning to fall into place as we continued to study His Word and confirm it through investigation of His scientific creation.

Once the beginning of the astronomical year has been established by using the vernal equinox, which always occurs around March 20, [17] as our guide, *then* we can determine the first day of our Creator's new year. Some people believe this new moon that marks the first day of Yahuweh's new year should be calculated by the new moon that occurs closest to the vernal equinox even if it occurs a few days *before* the equinox. This doesn't make sense. Because to use a new moon to mark the beginning of Yahuweh's new year *before* the vernal equinox puts the new moon (new month) in the old or previous year of the cycle of the sun, which ends as winter is ending. After much study, which includes the following verses, I believe the new moon that marks the first day of the first month has to occur *after* the vernal equinox.

> This new *moon* is the beginning of new *moons* for you, it is the first new *moon* of the year for you. (Exodus 12:2 ISR)

> Guard the new *moon* of Abib, and perform the Pesah, to יהוה your Elohim, for in the new *moon* of Abib יהוה your Elohim brought you out of Mitsrayim by night. (Deuteronomy 16:1 ISR)

That said, and once the vernal equinox has passed, we move on to how we now determine the new moon (new month) is oc-

---

17 Although striving to refrain from using the pagan names for the days of the week and months of the year in my spoken communication, the full spelling of these words will appear in written form.

curring. My friend shared that you can easily tell the beginning of a new moon, without the aid of NASA or other websites. Internet sites like NASA and the US Naval Observatory are technological conveniences we may not always have the privilege of referencing. So my friend taught me the following: "As you are seeing the last few days of the waning moon, where the sliver is growing smaller and smaller; get up around 5 a.m. and look in the eastern sky. It has to be dark. The waning sliver will appear lower and smaller each morning until you don't see it. On the morning that you don't see it and there is no more sliver, this "old" waning moon is gone. That evening you will not see a sliver in the western sky, and at sunset, you would call this "day one" of the new moon.

This is the conjunction that we are looking for in which the moon is dark, yet being renewed. Wikipedia says a lunar conjunction is an event where the Earth, moon, and sun (in that order) are approximately in a straight line. Preferably, you are able to observe these things in an open area that is not obstructed by city lights or tall buildings and trees. We are blessed to be in a small town, with it being easy to go to an elevated area not far from home.

For the previous six years, we had always determined the new moon by our own observation of the sliver, as well as by checking with others in our area and online to see if the sliver had been spotted. We would begin looking to the western sky and would see a very thin sliver of the moon after the sun had set. This was the best way at that time that we knew to determine a new moon. Now we believe this method is not as accurate, because seeing the sliver can mean a two- or three-day-old moon. I also discovered that the U.S. Naval Observatory defines a new moon as being in the dark (almost 0% illumination between waning and waxing). I shared my amazement at how this observatory defined a new moon with my friend. She said that science has always called the dark of the moon a "new moon," as scientists look for the beginning of a cycle and the end of a cycle of the moon and how it resets. A lunar cycle is approximately 29.5 days.

Again, in discussing with my friend the various ways that are used to figure the timing of a new moon, she said she had asked the Father, "Why are there no clear-cut instructions on how to carry out some of Your commands, especially having to do with determining when a new moon begins?" I asked her if He had given an answer. She replied, "I was impressed with this thought: it may be that our Heavenly Father wanted to see if we could 'hang tight' in the midst of indecisiveness and vagueness, and still love each other, even though we may disagree on exactly how to determine the start of His appointed times." We both agreed that this would definitely be a good reason as we continue our learning and strive to follow His commands.

Then I shared: *We are all on a learning path as to how to walk on His highway, coming from different directions, different life experiences, and different ways of learning that I like to call "our bent."* It is so wonderful to have a friend to study with and who likes to "dig into" the Scriptures, always searching for our Father's truths!

We talked about the importance of first loving Him with all our heart, trusting in the gift of His Son, and of having the fear of Him. He is the One to establish our way. My friend reminded me of the fact that the appointed times of the Feast of Yahuweh show a picture of what His Son has fulfilled and then of what He will do in fulfilling His Father's prophecies.

I know His Word says that even nature cries out as a witness of Him and that we are without excuse. So we look to the science of how the moon cycles. And from what I understand, when the lunar conjunction takes place, the moon begins to illuminate very quickly. Yet the sliver or crescent may not become visible for up to three days later because of the sun's brightness.

Strong's Concordance H2320 defines the word "*chodesh*" as new moon or month and notes that it is derived from Strong's H2318 "*chadash*," which means "to renew," just like the moon cycle is renewed each month. By contrast, Strong's H7720 "*saharon*" is Hebrew for "crescent," meaning a round pendant and round like the moon (also see H5469). Saharon is used only three times in the KJV, with each occurrence referring to pagan ornaments fashioned in honor and worship of the crescent moon. *Encyclopedia Britannica* online says that the crescent symbol is a political, military, and religious emblem of the Byzantine and Turkish empires (and later and more generally a symbol of all Islamic countries). So for all these reasons and more, Kevin, Mom, and I have moved away from using the sighting of the sliver (crescent) of the moon as a way of determining the new moon.

Another Scripture to ponder is 1 Samuel 20:5 and 18, where David and Jonathan knew that the next day was going to be the new moon. How did they know this ahead of time if they had to wait for reports of sightings of a visible sliver of the moon?

As stated above, first we have to know when the new year begins (vernal equinox), then we determine the new moon (month) by the conjunction; then we determine the day ("*yom*" in Hebrew) of the first appointed time of the year, which is Passover (*Pesah/Pesach* in Hebrew) because Scripture tells us the Passover occurs on the fourteenth day of the first new moon.

I want to include a side note here that many people celebrate the Passover according to man's calendar and according to the dates set by Jewish tradition and not by the timing that I just described. Although their declarations of the dates for the Passover each year are close to the way we now figure the timing of the Passover, and even sometimes fall at the same time, we have decided that we should only rely on Yahuweh's naturally occurring time systems of the moon and sun, just as Genesis 1:14 indicates. We had well-meaning Christian friends assume that we were celebrating on the Jewish calendar dates for Passover. But because it calculates our Father's appointed times well in advance of when the feast days should naturally occur and does not rely solely on the monthly cycles of the moon and the yearly cycle of the sun as they occur, we do not follow a traditional calendar. I understand the convenience of predetermining dates according to man's traditions, especially so that calendars can be printed and distributed far in advance, yet I do not believe that this is what our Father desires. After having said all this, I am grateful to see how our Heavenly Father is bringing us closer in many ways to our Jewish brothers and sisters simply by the fact that we are recognizing our need to keep our Father's feasts and many Jews are also coming to the realization of their need to recognize Yahushua as their Messiah.

Passover starts at sundown on the fourteenth day of the new month (new moon) of our Creator's new year. This is our starting point. And knowing when our Father's year starts (the first month of His Scriptural year), we are set for determining each successive numbered month, as well as the counting system our Father provides for determining Shavuot, which occurs in the early summer months. The fall appointed times (fall feast days) begin on the first day of the seventh month. Again, we believe it is best to determine the exact day of the seventh month just as we determine when each new moon starts—by the conjunction of the moon. The first day of the seventh new moon is very important as we are instructed to remember to blow a horn (render a shout) on this day, called "Feast of Trumpets." This day is also called "the day that no man knows." And this is true because we do not know that exact day each year as we wait and watch for the conjunction of the moon to know when the first day of the seventh month is. I go into greater detail in the following paragraphs concerning this annual appointed time.

Back to our discussion of Passover, here are some of the Scriptures about the different times and commands surrounding this feast: Exodus 12:1-11; Leviticus 23:4-5; Numbers 9:2-14, 28:16, and 33:3; Deuteronomy 16:1-7; Joshua 5:10-11; and 2 Kings 23:21-23.

There are varying practices today in the way people commemorate the Passover, including eating bitter herbs, standing and eating in haste, reading the different accounts of the Passover from Scripture, and serving a dish that includes lamb. But personally (first and foremost), we must set this day aside as a *set-apart gathering* as commanded in Leviticus 23:4. Then, specifically for Passover and the Feast of Unleavened Bread, we literally remove the leaven from our house as tangible reminders of getting the sin out of our lives. And as commanded, we eat unleavened bread for seven days as we feast symbolically on the unleavened bread of sincerity and truth. These commands were for all the citizenship of Israel as well as foreigners who dwelt among the Israelites and who were circumcised. And through Yahushua Messiah, we have been grafted into this citizenship, and our hearts have been circumcised. See Ephesians 2:10-13, 19. I know the command to be physically circumcised can be a hot topic of debate, especially around Passover (Exodus 12:48-49 and Numbers 9:14).

At the time of writing this book, I am not inspired to write an in-depth study of circumcision from the perspective of being able to eat the Passover meal or not. This is something each person needs to study, with the leading of the Set-apart Spirit of Truth. My advice, again, is that you dig for the answer, taking into account all the verses you can find concerning this subject, then look at them as a whole and not base any conclusion on just one or two verses. Our motive must always be that of wanting to please our Heavenly Father from *His* perspective and not from our own human perspective.

To date, we have personally chosen to keep the observance of the Passover very simple, not wanting to add any of the traditional "Jewish" customs (especially if they are not listed in the Torah). There is such a huge misconception that arises from calling the Father's commands "Jewish commands" when we honor His Sabbath on the seventh day and keep His festivals, which were designed for all mankind who will follow His Son and His Laws. Even the Pope calls these commands "the Jewish Sabbath" and "the Jewish feasts," which misleadingly labels anyone who keeps these commands as "Jewish" or "trying to be Jewish," and of even following Judaism. In the beginning we were told that we had discarded our "Savior, Jesus" because we were trying to obey the command to keep the Sabbath. We tried to witness that we would never let go of our belief and personal decision to follow Him. They could not hear our words and could not understand. So we had to be patient and just keep walking in His commands, praying that others would see we had not let go of our salvation and our witness of our faith in our Messiah by any means.

I can understand some of their misconceptions, as I have discussed in previous chapters, because it *was* to the Jews that Yahuweh's commands/Law/Torah were first written down and entrusted to Moses to deliver (Romans 3:1-2). And it is the Jewish race that has kept many of these commands throughout the ages. But now is the time for us to wake up and see that our Creator has the same design for everyone who will love Him and each other as He has had from the beginning.

A second reason we want to stay as close as we can to only following Yahuweh's written instructions concerning the keeping of His appointed times is because we still have much more to learn in knowing and following what our Father has outlined in His Word, as opposed to man's traditions and holidays that we had just come out of. Our personal experience of leaving behind man's traditions has left us very "gun-shy" of going back into any of man's other traditions, including Jewish traditions that are not commanded in the Scriptures, even if some of them do not go against His commands.

Getting back on track concerning the Passover, I find it interesting that there are only two verses in Leviticus 23 concerning this feast day. And Leviticus 23 does not contain the command to remove the leaven from the households as does Exodus 12:15, 13:7, and Deuteronomy 16:4. Again, it is not too much for us to physically remove the products containing leaven from our house before the Passover and during the Feast of Unleavened Bread as a tangible reminder that Yahushua cleansed the sin from our lives through His blood sacrifice at Passover. He is our unleavened (without sin) Bread of Life.

A side note that my friend pointed out to me is that "leaven" is not only symbolic of sin, but is also symbolic of false doctrine that we must rid ourselves of. Mark 8:15 and Matthew 16:11-12 discuss the leaven of the Pharisees and Sadducees (their doctrine in that day) and the leaven of Herod (the ruler of the day).

Of particular emphasis, I want to explain a very important matter concerning the commands for the observance of the Passover that were to be followed by His people during the time period between the Exodus from Egypt and the time of our Messiah's sacrifice. Beginning in Deuteronomy 16:2-7, Yahuweh states three times that the Passover lamb is to be slaughtered and eaten in the place *where He chooses to place His name*. Pesah is Passover and Mitsrayim is Egypt. To bring the slaughtered Pesah to the place "where His Name dwells," means to bring the slaughtered Pesah *to the priests*.

> And you shall slaughter the Pesah to יהוה your Elohim, from the flock and the herd, in the place

where יהוה chooses to put His Name. Eat no leavened bread with it. For seven days you eat unleavened bread with it, bread of affliction, because you came out of the land of Mitsrayim in haste—so that you remember the day in which you came out of the land of Mitsrayim, all the days of your life. And no leaven should be seen with you in all your border for seven days, neither should *any* of the meat which you slaughter in the evening on the first day stay all night until morning. You are not allowed to slaughter the Pesah within any of your gates which יהוה your Elohim gives you, but at the place where יהוה your Elohim chooses to make His Name dwell, there you slaughter the Pesah in the evening, at the going down of the sun, at the appointed time you came out of Mitsrayim. (Deuteronomy 16:2-7 ISR)

As we were studying this passage, we wondered *where did Yahuweh choose to put His name?* The answer is found in 1 Kings 8:16-20 and 29, 44. He chooses to put His name in Jerusalem. It would be good to read all of 1 Kings Chapter 8 to get a clearer picture of the importance of Yahuweh's name and of how He chose to place His name in the house that King Solomon built for Him in Jerusalem.

And Leviticus 17:1-9 also gives a stern warning for anyone who slaughters an animal *and does not bring it before the priests* at the door of the Tent of Appointment, which was during the time of sojourning in the wilderness.

So to date, we continue to find evidence in Scripture that we are *not* to perform animal sacrifices or slaughterings for the Passover, not even for remembrance sake. The above verses are clear instructions for Yahuweh's people to commemorate *after* their Exodus from Egypt and *includes* the required presence of the Levitical priesthood. And the first Passover that occurred on the night *before* the exodus was a unique time in which Ya-huweh had each family use lamb's blood on their door posts so He would pass over and protect His people from the curse of death of the first-born. Yet there are still some who, I believe, mistakenly think that in trying to obey our Creator's commands, we have the ability and even the obligation to continue shedding blood, in particular a lamb or a goat, to *commemorate* the Pass-over in this day and time, which is *after* our Messiah's sacrifice that takes away the sins of the world.

> Therefore cleanse out the old leaven, so that you are a new lump, as you are unleavened. For also Messiah our Pesah was slaughtered for us. So then let us celebrate the festival, not with old leaven, nor with the leaven of evil and wickedness, but with the unleavened bread of sincerity and truth. (1 Corinthians 5:7-8 ISR)

And Paul tells the Corinthians of how he learned the following:

> For I received from the Master that which I also delivered to you: that the Master יהושע, in the night that He was delivered up took bread, and having given thanks, He broke it and said, 'Take, eat, this is My body which is broken for you; do this in remembrance of Me.' In the same way also the cup, after supper, saying, "This cup is the renewed covenant in My blood. As often as you drink it, do this in remembrance of Me." For as often as you eat this bread and drink this cup, you proclaim the death of the Master until He comes. (1 Corinthians 11:23-26 ISR)

The blood of our Savior has been shed for our sins, He

LENORA HOAG

has replaced, with His own blood, the shedding of blood from animals.

> For it is impossible for blood of bulls and goats to take away sins. Therefore, coming into the world, He says, "Slaughtering and meal offering You did not desire, but a body You have prepared for Me. (Hebrews 10:4-5 ISR)

And the following verse is one that is mistakenly used to say that now we are our own priests to justify killing an animal for Passover. But being "a royal priesthood" does not mean we are a Levitical priesthood and are to perform their duties. Yahushua Messiah is the high priest according to the order of Malkitsedeq, which is a *royal* priesthood. There could be a long discussion here concerning the order of Malkitsedeq and of how it is different from the Levitical priesthood, especially in that it is "royal" and the Levitical priesthood is *not* "royal." The book of Hebrews is a good started to understanding the Malkitsedeq priesthood.

> But you are a chosen race, a royal priesthood, a set-apart nation, a people for a possession, that you should proclaim the praises of Him who called you out of darkness into His marvelous light, who once were not a people, but now the people of Elohim, who had not obtained compassion, but now obtained compassion. (1 Peter 2:9-10 ISR)

Now, moving from our discussion of Passover on the fourteenth day of the new moon, the next appointed time is the Feast of Unleavened Bread (Matzot). It begins the very next day after Passover on the fifteenth day of this new moon *at sundown on the fourteenth* (also called the month of Abib). On the first and seventh days of this weeklong appointed time, there is to be a set-apart gathering and no servile work is to be done.

And on the fifteenth day of this new *moon* is the

Festival of Matzot to יהוה —seven days you eat unleavened bread. 'On the first day you have a set-apart gathering; you do no servile work. And you shall bring an offering made by fire to יהוה for seven days. On the seventh day is a set-apart gathering; you do no servile work.' (Leviticus 23:6-8 ISR)

Again, the basics for the first and the seventh days of the Feast of Unleavened Bread are to do no work, to have a set-apart gathering, and to eat unleavened bread on days one through seven of this feast.

We knew in the beginning of our learning about the Feast days that it was easy to see we were not to eat any leavened bread or anything with leaven in it for seven days. And we also learned about the command to physically remove leaven from our houses too, as a literal act to represent how our Messiah removes "sin" from our lives. Leaven is a food product that makes food rise—products like yeast, baking powder, or baking soda. It's easy to think that this was just for back then, but this is one of those commands that we can do today that if at all possible should be completed.

> In the first month you are to eat unleavened bread, from the evening of the fourteenth day until the evening of the twenty-first day. For seven days there must be no leaven found in your houses. If anyone eats something leavened, that person, whether a foreigner or native of the land, must be cut off from the congregation of Israel. You are not to eat anything leavened; eat unleavened bread in all your homes. (Exodus 12:18-20 Berean Study Bible)

Also see Exodus 13:7-10 and 1 Corinthians 5:8 (symbolic and literal).

We didn't realize until later that the Scriptures were also telling us *to eat* unleavened bread for seven days to commemorate the Passover. We are always learning.

> You shall not eat leavened bread with it; for seven days you shall eat unleavened bread with it. (Deuteronomy 16:3a NASB).

The book of Numbers also shows this same command:

> On the fifteenth day of this month *there shall be* a feast; unleavened bread shall be eaten for seven days. (Numbers 28:17 NASB)

Remember in the above paragraphs where I mentioned that it was interesting to me that out of all of Yahuweh's appointed times that are listed in Leviticus chapter 23, the Passover only has two verses describing this very important set-apart time? I think that I may have discovered a reason for this. When Yahuweh first gave these laws in written form to His people through Moses, He was looking ahead in time and planning His instructions for the time when the Passover sacrifice would change from shedding the blood of lambs and goats to the shed blood of His Son. Therefore, He purposely did not give all the detailed instructions for the killing and preparation of the animals that He gave in Exodus 12:1-11; Numbers 9:2-14, 28:16, and 33:3; and Deuteronomy 16:1-7.

He also indicates that His laws are forever and that we are to complete them even today. So it makes sense that in this particular chapter of Leviticus 23 that gives such an excellent overview of all His appointed, set-apart times, that the verses detailing the specifics of the Passover are brief and generalized.

We also discussed in previous chapters that there are still some never-ending commands we cannot however complete because of the day and time and under the governments that we now live. In determining which commands we can keep, like the physical removal of leaven from our homes, it may appear silly or nonessential to some, yet, it is a never-ending command we *can* complete without going against any of His other commands and without going against any present-day laws of the land in which we are living. I am so often reminded of the instruction to "study" His Word in order to rightly divide it, to know how and when to use it in our lives.

Now moving from Leviticus 23:6-8 concerning the Feast of Unleavened Bread, the next verses in this chapter, beginning with verses 9 through 13, contain the command to bring a sheaf of the first fruits of harvest *to the priest* for a wave offering. There is also a sacrifice of a male lamb, a year old, a perfect one for an ascending offering and a grain offering with its drink offering of wine. These specific commands required the Levitical priesthood, and we do not perform their priestly duties today. Yet it is still important to study these verses to understand what was commanded by our Heavenly Father, as we determine the start of the *omer count* to know when Shavout (Pentacost) is to be observed each year. This is another area in which there is a difference in how believers do their figuring.

Look carefully at Leviticus 23:14 as it commands the Israelites to not eat bread or roasted grain or fresh grain until the same day that the sheaf of the wave offering is brought.

> And you do not eat bread or roasted grain or fresh grain until the same day that you have brought an offering to your Elohim—a law forever throughout your generations in all your dwellings. (Leviticus 23:14 ISR)

At first, we believed this verse was significant in telling us not to eat leavened bread, thus making the count for Shavuot to not begin until *after* the completion of the Feast of Unleavened Bread. To date, after more study (both personally and with friends), we now believe this verse is referring only to the new harvest, which would have been the barley harvest. The waving of the first sheaf is symbolic of our Messiah being the first-fruits offering when He arose on the first day of the week *during* the Feast of Unleavened Bread. Therefore, the Omer count that is to begin as "day one" and takes place on the same day that the first sheaf of the barley harvest is waved, is the first day of the week (the day after the seventh-day Sabbath) during the Feast of Unleavened Bread.

> And from the morrow after the Sabbath, from the day that you brought the sheaf of the wave offering, you shall count for yourselves: seven completed Sabbaths. (Leviticus 23:15 ISR)

And in the very next verse, Yahuweh gives a second way to count the omer:

> Until the morrow after the seventh Sabbath you count fifty days, then you shall bring a new grain offering to יהוה. (Leviticus 23:16 ISR)

Therefore, to the best of our knowledge to date, we believe that the Omer count starts and continues seven Sabbaths from the specific day after the Sabbath when Yahushua arose.

The next verses of Leviticus 23:17-20 are instructions involving the priest. However, when you get to verse 21, you find an instruction that *we can keep,* which is for us to have a set-apart gathering and to rest from our labors on Shavuot.

As I stated above, Shavout is the same day as Pentecost and is significant to all believers because it is the same day that the disciples received the Set-apart Spirit. Many people are told that Shavuot is a Jewish holiday, while Pentecost is a Christian holiday. But I call them what they are: Yahuweh's appointed times. And on this date is a set-apart, commanded gathering, originated and ordained by our Creator. Shavuot is the day He gave His Law to Moses in written form on Mt. Sinai. And it is the same day Yahuweh gave His Set-apart Spirit to the early believers in Jerusalem. Pentecost is from the Greek "*petekostos*," which means "fifty." Fifty days is the "omer" count of how to determine when Shavuot is to be observed.

In my research, I found that determining the count for the omer is a 2300-year-old debate that began in the different sects of Jewish leaders before our Messiah was crucified. And now, as we are waking up to the everlasting commands of our Heavenly Father, we, too, are trying to be as obedient and true to our Maker's instructions as possible.

Our Creator does not include random information in His Word. There is usually more than one reason why a detail or details are given. And the manner in which they are given (the order of the details and their repetition) is very important. I have been at a loss more than once as I read His Word. But, if I diligently keep on asking and searching for His wisdom to honor Him to the best of my ability, in His timing, He will reveal His truth and will not disappoint.

Finally, we are getting to discuss the last three appointed times (often called the fall feasts).

> And יהוה spoke to Mosheh, saying, 'Speak to the children of Yisra'el, saying, "In the seventh new *moon*, on the first day of the new *moon*, you have a rest, a remembrance of Teru'ah, a set-apart gathering. You do no servile work, and you shall bring an offering made by fire to יהוה"' (Leviticus 23: 23-25 ISR)

This is another appointment with our Father in which we are to have a gathering that is set apart. At first, I kept wondering what do the words "bring an offering made by fire" mean? I thought there may be something symbolically we were supposed to do in place of these burnt offerings, even though I knew the tasks of these offerings are specific to the Levitical priesthood. I also knew that Psalm 27:6 speaks of offering a slaughter (sacrifice) of praise with our voice. And I remembered Hebrews 13:15 encourages us, through Yahushua Messiah, to continually offer to Yahuweh a sacrifice of praise, the fruit of our lips (giving praise to His Name). Again, it's good to read the various translations of this verse. So for now, I believe we should follow the examples and the leading of these two references in singing and speaking praises as our offerings/sacrifices.

Teru'ah in Hebrew is defined in Strong's H8643 as "a shout or blast of war, alarm, or joy."

> And in the day of your gladness, and in your appointed times, and at the beginning of your new *moons*, you shall blow the trumpets over your ascending offerings and over your slaughterings of peace *offerings*. And they shall be a remembrance for you before your Elohim. I am יהוה your Elohim. (Numbers 10:10 ISR)

Notice the word "remembrance." The blowing of the shofar must have a specific significance in our future if we are supposed to remember to do it throughout our generations.

A blast, shout, blowing of a horn are all descriptive of either a trumpet or a ram's horn. Look at Strong's H7782, which is "*shofar*." In the beginning, we realized we could easily obey this command; the first year we went outside on the evening of the Feast of Trumpets and shouted praises with our voice. We didn't have a horn. The next year, we ordered a small ram's horn from Israel, which was about $20. It came with a small instruction booklet, which was interesting as we learned how to make the sound of different trumpet blasts.

Again, to determine when the new moon of each month is occurring, including the seventh month for these fall feast days, you can use NASA, the U.S. Naval Observatory, and other websites. And you can refer back to the beginning of this section where I discussed how we confirm the beginning of a new moon by knowing the conjunction phase (when the moon has gone dark).

Scripture does not have many instructions for the Feast of Trumpets other than blowing the shofar, doing no servile work, and having a set-apart gathering on the first day of this seventh new moon. However, when reading about trumpet blasts throughout the Old and New Testaments, especially the prophecies given by Yahushua in the gospels, and the prophecies containing these blasts or shouts in Revelation, we can see this is a very important day, as these blasts signify that people should take notice and come together. We believe that this very important feast is a picture of the future gathering of believers in Messiah at His return. We are watching and waiting.

The next appointed time that you will soon see that our Heavenly Father is extremely serious about, is called Yom haKippurim, or Day of Atonement. It occurs on the tenth day of the seventh month that began with the Feast of Trumpets. Read very carefully all of the following verses.

Notice the repetition and detailed instructions that Yahuweh gave.

> And יהוה spoke to Mosheh, saying, 'On the tenth day of this seventh new *moon* is Yom haKippurim. It shall be a set-apart gathering for you. And you shall afflict your beings, and shall bring an offering made by fire to יהוה and you do no work on that same day, for it is Yom Kiippurim, to make atonement for you before יהוה your Elohim. For any being who is not afflicted on that same day, he shall be cut off from his people. And any being who does any work on that same day, that being I shall destroy from the midst of his people. You do no work—a law forever throughout your generations in all your dwellings. It is a Sabbath of rest to you, and you shall afflict your

beings. On the ninth day of the new *moon* at evening, from evening to evening, you observe your Sabbath.' (Leviticus 23:26-32 ISR)

Do you see how serious our Heavenly Father is, especially when He tells us three times that we must not do any work on this day? The day of Atonement (Yom haKippurim) is the next-to-the-last appointed time of the year, just before the Feast of Tabernacles (Sukkot). And all three of the fall Feast days not only reflect our Messiah and past events but also point us to future events and what must take place when He returns. I believe that the significance of the Day of Atonement represents the final fulfillment of our salvation just prior to our being able to celebrate and tabernacle with our Messiah at His return. (1 Thessalonians Chapters 4 and 5)

What do you think "afflict your being" means? We know that many people afflict their being or soul on this day by fasting.

But I think it means more than that. Look at several translations of Leviticus 23:27 on Biblehub.com at **https://biblehub.com/leviticus/23-27.htm** and notice the words they use, including the word "afflict." They use "humble" and "deny your being." Strong's definition says this word in Hebrew is *"anah"* (H6031), which means "defile," as in to humble oneself before the Father. We are to humble our being (soul). How does one do this? Spiritually, to humble our being is to deny ourselves as our Messiah commanded in Matthew 16:24. And physically, we can fast for twenty-four hours on this day from food and water as queen Esther did, in addition to crying out to our Heavenly Father in His Son's Name, and to ask as King David did, "Father, is there any hurtful way in me?" We use common sense to consider the needs of children, the elderly, and anyone with health issues.

During our twenty-four-hour fast, we wait—quietly, humbly, and privately—as we lay our souls bare before Him. We see the day of Yom haKippurim (Day of Atonement) not as a celebratory gathering, but as a solemn soul-searching gathering. I know it's a little hard to privately "soul search" while with a group of people. But wherever you may be gathering, and depending on the number of people and the space, there can be a time of sitting alone, quietly, before Yahuweh—a special time allotted during your gathering. Then, collectively, there can be times of Scripture reading and prayer, too. There is a prayer that lends itself well to a group setting when read in unison or in taking turns—Daniel 9:3-19. It is Daniel's cry, confessing his sins and the sins of his people, Israel. He is laying his soul bare in seeking Yahuweh by prayer and supplication, with fasting, sackcloth, and ashes. It is a desperate and beautiful prayer, and to me a good example, of afflicting our being. Ever since I heard this prayer, as we first read it together in a small group setting, I never forgot it. The following words at the beginning and the end of Daniel's prayer touch my heart:

> We have sinned and did crookedness, and did wrong and rebelled, to turn aside from Your commands and from Your right-rulings. And we have not listened to Your servants the prophets, who spoke in Your Name to our sovereigns, our heads, and our fathers, and to all the people of the land. (Daniel 9:5-6 ISR)

If we are honest, we will especially realize that in this day and age, we have sinned, and done wrong, and turned away from our Creator and His ways.

Look at how Daniel ends his prayer, as I do believe we could very well cry out in the same way:

> O יהוה, hear! O יהוה, forgive! O יהוה, listen and act! Do not delay for Your own sake, my Elohim, for Your city and Your people are called by Your Name. (Daniel 9:19 ISR)

The next feast of Yahuweh's appointed times occurs five days later, after the Day of Atonement.

And יהוה spoke to Mosheh, saying, 'Speak to the children of Yisra'el, saying, 'On the fifteenth day of this seventh new moon is the Festival ofSukkot for seven days to יהוה. On the first day is a set-apart gathering; you do no servile work. For seven days you bring an offering made by fire to יהוה. On the eighth day there shall be a set-apart gathering for you, and you shall bring an offering made by fire to יהוה. It is a closing festival; you do no servile work. These are the appointed times of יהוה which you proclaim as set-apart gatherings, to bring an offering made by fire to יהוה, an ascending offering and a grain offering, a slaughtering and drink offering, as commanded for every day—besides the Sabbaths of יהוה, and besides your gifts, and besides all your vows, and besides all your voluntary offerings which you give to יהוה. On the fifteenth day of the seventh new *moon*, when you gather in the fruit of the land, celebrate the festival of יהוה for seven days. On the first day is a rest, and on the eighth day a rest. And you shall take for yourselves on the first day the fruit of good trees, branches of palm trees, twigs of leafy trees, and willows of the stream, and shall rejoice before יהוה your Elohim for seven days. And you shall celebrate it as a festival to יהוה for seven days in the year—a law forever in your generations. Celebrate it in the seventh new *moon*. Dwell in booths for seven days; all who are native born in Yisra'el dwell in booths, so that your generations know that I made the children of Yisra'el dwell in booths when I brought them out of the land of Mitsrayim. I am

יהוה your Elohim. Thus did Mosheh speak of the appointed times of יהוה to the children of Yisra'el. (Leviticus 23:33-44 ISR)

Sukkot is plural for "booths," and *sukkah* is singular for "booth." A booth is a temporary dwelling or shelter. Strong's H5521 "*sukkah*" is defined as "a thicket, booth." Other definitions are "canopy," "pavilion," "hut," "lair." Also notice Leviticus 23:34 and 23:39 above having the same wording: "on the fifteenth day of the seventh new *moon*." Verse 34 says this day is the beginning of the Festival of Sukkoth (Booths) for seven days of celebration. And verse 39 says this fifteenth day is the day when the fruit of the land is gathered in. I am still learning what all of this means, especially prophetically, as most of us are not personally growing crops.

I know there are those who have read, researched, and had insights revealed to them who are sharing the prophetic meaning of Yahuweh's appointed times. And I have witnessed over the past twenty years the increasing practice of even mainstream Christian leaders and preachers teaching the significance of at least knowing about Yahuweh's feasts in light of their fulfillment of prophecy. Although I love to search for the symbolic and deeper meanings of Yahuweh's words, I have not focused extensively on the prophetic meanings and implications of each of His appointed times for the writing of this book. There is already a lot of this type of teaching out there. But remember, as with all teachings: test everything against His Word and with the leading of the Set-apart Spirit.

The focus of this book is to prayerfully dispel some of the lies and misinterpretations we have inherited concerning Yahweh's Word. Whatever you read or hear concerning future prophecy, as connected to the continuation of the appointed times of Yahuweh, remember most of all His Son's teachings, especially in Matthew 5:17-18: "Not one jot and not one tittle will pass from the Law until heaven and Earth pass away." And the feasts and Sabbath are contained within the Law. I take Yahushua's words literally and prophetically to mean, even in His millennial reign, that not one jot or one tittle will pass from the Law, because heaven and Earth will still be in existence at that time.

Zechariah 14 is an example of the Feast of Sukkot (Feast of Tabernacles) continuing in the millennial kingdom. I have seen in Scripture where it looks as if the Levitical priesthood may be reinstated after Yahushua sets up His earthly kingdom as well as a slaughter place being set up during this time. But for sure, I know His feast days are commanded for all of Yahuweh's people, no matter the period of time in history in which they live. I have quoted these verses before, but they are so important and eye-opening that I want to repeat them here:

> All of you are standing here today before יהוה your Elohim: your leaders, your tribes, your elders and your officers, all the men of Yisra'el, your little ones, your wives, and your sojourner who is in the midst of your camp, from the one who cuts your wood to the one who draws your water, so that you should enter into covenant with יהוה your Elohim, and into His oath, which יהוה your Elohim makes with you today, in order to establish you today as a people for Himself, and He Himself be your Elohim, as He has spoken to you, and as He has sworn to your fathers, to Abraham, to Yitshaq, and to Ya'aqob. 'And not with you alone I am making this covenant and this oath, but with him who stands here with us today before יהוה our Elohim, as well as with him who is not here with us today. (Deuteronomy 29:10-15 ISR)

Did you see the very specific, detailed description of who was present at this meeting, from the elders and officers and all the men of Israel to the women and children and sojourners?

Then in verse 14, Yahuweh is speaking directly to this large group. And He makes it a point to say that He is not only making a covenant with this particular gathering of Israel, but He wants them to know that this covenant of *establishing a people for Himself* goes further, to those who are not standing with them on that day. This speaks volumes to me as I can see that this means our Maker was talking to us and including us (a people yet to be born) when He was talking to the first people He called "His." This next verse also confirms this thought for me. Paul wrote this to the Romans as he was quoting what the Father said in Hosea 2:23:

> ...I will call those who were not my people, 'my people,' and her who was not beloved, 'beloved.' (Romans 9:25 NASB)

We are still learning how to celebrate *to Yahuweh* during the festival of Sukkot. I have been blessed in being able, the last two years, to camp briefly with my friend Peggy in her little camper at state parks here in Texas. Because of family needs, especially in caring for our elderly mothers, Kevin and I have not been able to celebrate Sukkot together by camping with others or even camping anywhere but in our trailer at our house. And we love to camp! When our children were young, we camped all around Texas, no matter how hot or cold the weather was. We pray to be able to get back to it soon. And there are grandkids now to make camping memories with!

During Sukkot, I understand there are numerous celebrations across the country at lakes, parks, private properties, etc., where like-minded believers get together during this wonderful fall festival. It's easy to find these groups if you just do an online search with the word Feast of Tabernacles or Sukkot and the present year.

During this fall festival, some even build a *sukkah* (a temporary three- or four-sided hut or lean-to) in which they fellowship, read, and eat their meals. Again, the most important place to start in keeping Yahuweh's appointed times is to set His commanded days of rest apart from our work and to gather with like-minded and like-hearted individuals who are humbly learning how to obey Yahuweh's commands through the saving forgiveness and power of His Son. It does not matter the size of the group, whether it is big or small.

Now, in looking at the last few verses of Leviticus 23, I want to discuss an area that I really had to study. Several years ago, Kevin and I really questioned what "native born in Yisra'el" means in the following verse:

> Dwell in booths for seven days, all who are native born in Yisra'el dwell in booths. (Leviticus 23:42 ISR)

We know that physically we are not "native born." And Kevin and I do not get into the genealogy, DNA, and ancestry queries even though this has become very popular. But after studying Ephesians 2:10-13 and 19, Romans 11:24, and the verses I quoted above where Yahuweh addresses His people "Is-rael" (before they went into the promised land), we know that we have become as "native born." Our hearts have been circumcised through His Son in order to then obey His commands. Therefore, we too are His people that He calls "Israel."

> And when a stranger sojourns with you and shall perform the Pesah to יהוה let all his males be circumcised, and then let him come near and perform it, and he shall be as a native of the land. But let no uncircumcised eat of it. There is one Torah for the native-born and for the stranger who sojourns among you. (Exodus 12:48-49 ISR)

We know the most important inheritance we could possibly receive is to be included in Yahuweh's Kingdom as we have already discussed that through Yahushua Messiah we are grafted into the citizenship of Israel. And today, Yahuweh is bringing His people from both groups (Christians and Jews) as I shared in the early chapters of this book—Christians are waking up to Yahuweh's commands and Jews are waking up in large numbers to the saving favor of Yahushua Messiah. We are being formed into "one house," that spiritual house of Israel, of which our Heavenly Father says, "these are My people." His people know His voice and His voice is spoken through His Word and His Son—both His Word and His Son simultaneously reflect the keeping of His set-apart appointed times.

And these set-apart times are everlasting appointments with Him throughout history on into the tribulation as shown in the prophecy of Daniel:

> He will speak out against the Most High and oppress the saints of the Most High, intending to change the appointed times and the laws; and the saints will be given into his hand for a time, and times, and half a time. (Daniel 7:25 Berean Study Bible)

So I ask, upon discovering that your Maker's set-apart appointed times are meant for you as a believer, will you then learn to follow them to the best of your ability?

CHAPTER 16

*What if you realized your Maker is
pointing you in a different direction
than the way you have been going?*

H OW DO YOU TURN AROUND? Who do you trust?
What do you believe?

Our Heavenly Father speaks through His Set-apart
Spirit of Truth, calling us back to Him, to the direction and purpose in which we were created. And He gave us His commands
in **His Word** to direct even the smallest details of our lives, from
what we eat to who we spend our time with. He longs for us
to let Him be intimately involved through our obedience to His
design for living and loving Him and others.

Just like a child needs its father, He wants us to love and
trust, need and respect Him. Above all, He wants our heart.

When a child asks: Why did the Creator make people?

Simply answer: to love Him and for Him to love them.

Why does He want people to obey His commands?

To protect them and for them to show Him love.

What happens when people don't obey His commands?

They get hurt.

This is why He made us, and this is why we live. It's as
simple as that! Every human being is born with the purpose to be

with their Creator, to walk humbly with Him, but we got separated. And only one path can lead us home. We start our journey with His Son. In John 3:16 and 14:6 it tells us our Maker loved us so much that He gave His only begotten Son as a ransom for us. And that His Son is the one path, the only way back, to a pure and righteous Creator.

On this journey the next step is like a young child just learning to walk. Guided by the Set-apart Spirit that we received when we repented of our sins and believed in His Son, we humbly and fearfully follow what He shows us one step at a time. Look at this heartfelt prayer of King David's that we could all pray:

> ⁵ I acknowledged my sin to You, and my crookedness I did not hide. I have said, "I confess my transgressions to יהוה, You forgave the crookedness of my sin. Selah. ⁶ Therefore, let every lovingly-committed one pray to You while *You* might be found; even in a flood of great waters they would not reach him. ⁷ You are my hiding place; You preserve me from distress; You surround me with songs of deliverance. Selah. ⁸ 'Let Me instruct you and teach you in the way you should go; let Me counsel, My eye be on you. ⁹ Do not be like the horse, like the mule, with no understanding, with bit and bridle, else they do not come near you.' ¹⁰ Many are the sorrows of the wrong; but as for the one trusting in יהוה, loving-commitment surrounds him. ¹¹ Be glad in יהוה and exult, you righteous; and shout for joy, all you upright in heart! (Psalm 32:5-11 ISR)

Did you notice the switch in verse 8 and 9 from David's petition to Yahuweh petitioning David with His answer? Yahuweh asks that we "let" Him instruct, teach, and counsel us. Trusting Him and being surrounded by our Father's loving commitment is a daily and lifelong experience of letting Him instruct us as we humbly and fearfully learn where and how He wants us to walk.

Also, David uses the word "Selah" twice during this prayer. It means, according to the Strong's Concordance, *to lift up, to exalt*. I think of "Selah" as an intended pause at the end of these thoughts in order to contemplate, "lift up," and let his words "soak in" before going on to the next thought.

Using His Word as our guide, Kevin, Mother, and I would humbly and fearfully obey what was being revealed to us, one step at a time. And many times, not realizing that as we obeyed, He would open up our understanding of another truth in how to please Him. This is how it all started when we discovered that Christmas was pagan. We had no idea that being obedient in this one matter would lead us to where we are today. And He continues to reveal deeper meanings hidden in His Word, making us closer to Him and His Son than we have ever been in our lives! And I know that if you humbly keep on searching for your Heavenly Father too, He will not let you down. It is a beautiful intimate walk between a loving Father, His Son, and their people.

As I shared in previous chapters, especially in Chapter 2 concerning the Sabbath, it wasn't always easy to change and follow His commands, but in doing so, the benefits cannot be measured. I also touched on the following insights in Chapter 2 but want to reiterate them here. Scripture defines scripture. And Isaiah 58:13-14 gives insight and definition to Psalm 37:4, quoted next.

Look at the following two quotes about the Sabbath and notice the words "delight yourself in יהוה." Then see the same words in the next quote of Psalm 37:4:

> If you do turn back your foot from the Sabbath, from doing your pleasure on My set-apart *day*, and shall call the Sabbath 'a delight,' the set-apart day of יהוה , 'esteemed,' and shall esteem it, not doing your own ways, nor finding your own pleasure, nor speaking

your own words, then you shall delight yourself in
יהוה. And I shall cause you to ride on the heights
of the earth, and feed you with the inheritance of
Ya'aqob your father. For the mouth of יהוה has
spoken! (Isaiah 58:13-14 ISR)

And delight yourself in יהוה and let Him give you
the desires of your heart. (Psalm 37:4 ISR)

You see that keeping the Sabbath (according to Isaiah) is
equal to delighting ourselves in Yahuweh. And when we delight
ourselves in Yahuweh, we are then in a position to get the desires
of our heart. The Sabbath is an appointment with our Creator, to
know Him, and to be on the same page as He is—our desires will
be His desires. And then, why wouldn't He give us the desires of
our hearts?

This is why He wants us to love and trust Him with *all* our
heart, to lay down our lives, to die daily to our own flesh, and
to be willing to put pleasing Him before pleasing ourselves and
even before pleasing our family. Are we willing to trust Him
that much? His Scriptures and His Son indicate that it is worth
it. And this is why He gives commands for every aspect of our
existence from who we love to how we celebrate and worship
and even to how we speak and work, to what we eat and how we
dress. Because of this intimate and incredible love He has for us,
He wants to be involved in every detail of our lives. He looks at
each person as if they were the only one walking around on the
face of this planet. He watches over every move we make, every
word we speak:

You know my sitting down and my rising up; You
understand my thought from afar. You sift my path
and my lying down, And know well all my ways. For
there is not a word on my tongue, But see, O יהוה,
You know it all! (Psalm 139:2-4 ISR)

He even counts every hair on our head:

> But even the very hairs of your head are all numbered.
> (Luke 12:7 KJV)

And He is so close and understanding of all our pain, He even collects our tears.

> You have counted my wanderings; You put my tears into Your bottle; are they not in Your book? (Psalm 56:8 ISR)

Do you see how loving, detailed, all-encompassing, jealous, set-apart, like-no-other Elohim He is? He wants His children (His people) to love Him with *all* their being and to be set-apart with Him! He went to great lengths to reach down and save us. And with all this love that He has for us, it was never meant to be a one-sided relationship. By now you know that He expects our part in loving Him to be in obeying His commands. We have this responsibility. And in the end, He will hold each of us accountable for the choice we made.

> By this we know that we love the children of Elohim, when we love Elohim and guard His commands. For this is the love for Elohim, that we guard His commands, and His commands are not heavy. (1 John 5:2-3 ISR)

If we are truly in the latter days, we have precious little time to turn back to Him, to give Him all of our heart.

And you shall love יהוה your Elohim with all your heart, and with all your being, and with all your might. And these Words which I am commanding you today shall be in your heart, and you shall impress them upon your children, and shall speak of them when you sit in your house, and when you walk by the way, and when you lie down, and when you rise up, and shall bind them as a sign on your hand, and they shall be as frontlets between your eyes. And you shall write them on the doorposts of your house and on your gates. (Deuteronomy 6:5-9 ISR)

And think of how different our homes would be, filled with His words of wisdom and love, if we literally took His commandments to heart, reading and teaching them to each other and to our children.

In these rapidly changing times, can we really afford to continue to be complacent to His instructions? Are we too busy to stop and learn His ways? I know personally that it's all too easy to completely fill our lives with work and even entertainment, leaving out even the thought of our Creator and His Son. How often do we pause to reflect on just exactly how and where we are spending our time in this life and to contemplate the direction in which we are going? Remember the truth I mentioned earlier about prioritizing our time that you always have time for what you put first?

It's important that we strive to prioritize this relationship with our Maker, getting to know Him, learning what pleases Him and what hurts and angers Him. We must be humble (poor in spirit), not stubborn in spirit.

> Today, if you hear His voice, do not harden your hearts as in the rebellion. (Psalms 95:7b-8a *and* Hebrews 3:15b ISR)

The fear of our Maker, which is giving Him the most awesome respect that we dare not go against Him, is the beginning of wisdom.

And King Solomon, after much searching, wrote the following about fearing our Maker at the very end of his writings in the book of Ecclesiastes:

> Let us hear the conclusion of the entire matter: Fear Elohim and guard His commands, for this *applies* to all mankind! For Elohim shall bring every work

into right-ruling, including all that is hidden whether good or whether evil. (Ecclesiastes 12:13-14 ISR)

It takes humility to fear Him. It takes humility to be teachable and let Him lead us in the way He wants us to go. And we must never stop learning, as we continue on this journey, if we want all the good that He has waiting for us. The following verse is also true for all of us, not just for a young man:

How can a young man keep his way pure? With all my heart I have sought You; Do not let me wander from Your commandments. (Psalm 119:9-10 NASB)

It is crucial for our eternity, as well as for our future generations that we walk in truth and not in deceit. Our Heavenly Father desires that none of us should perish.

But, beloved ones, let not this one *matter* be hidden from you: that with יהוה one day is as a thousand years, and a thousand years as one day. יהוה is not slow in regard to the promise, as some count slowness, but is patient toward us, not wishing that any should perish but that all should come to repentance. But the day of יהוה shall come as a thief in the night, in which the heavens shall pass away with a great noise, and the elements shall melt with intense heat, and the earth, and the works that are in it shall be burned up. (2 Peter 3:8-10 ISR)

The master of lies—the prince of this world, Satan—weaves his web, mixing truth with wrong conclusions and misperceptions to ever so cleverly make us believe we were destined to walk the paths that in all actuality belong to him and his servants! And he makes us believe that we shouldn't or even cannot overcome our fleshly desires. He convinces us that we have a right to pursue those desires and that they are our destiny! This kind of thinking takes the whole concept of being able to choose our Heavenly Father as master away from us!

> Do you not know that to whom you present yourselves servants for obedience, you are servants of the one whom you obey, whether of sin to death, or of obedience to righteousness? But thanks to Elohim that you were servants of sin, yet you obeyed from the heart that form of teaching to which you were entrusted. And having been set free from sin, you became servants of righteousness. I speak as a man, because of the weakness of your flesh. For even as you did present your members as servants of uncleanness, and of lawlessness resulting in lawlessness, so now present your members as servants of righteousness resulting in set-apartness. For when you were servants of sin, you were free from righteousness. What fruit, therefore, were you having then, over which you are now ashamed? For the end thereof is death. But now, having been set free from sin, and having become servants of Elohim, you have your fruit resulting in set-apartness, and the end, everlasting life. For the wages of sin is death, but the favourable gift of Elohim is everlasting life in Messiah יהושע our Master. (Romans 6:16-23 ISR)

It is a fact that we *do* serve a master, but it is also true that we get to choose our master, and in choosing, we will walk as *that* master has designed. This is the way that we were created—to submit to and serve one of two kingdoms, giving one of them our loyalty and our allegiance. We can't serve both. Our Messiah says:

> Whoever is not with me is against me, and whoever does not gather with me scatters. (Matthew 12:30 NIV)

You see, there is no in-between. We only have one of two choices. Obedient to sin or obedient to righteousness—that's our only two choices. Remember there are no gray areas in this. And His Law *is* His design that gives us the definition of exactly what sin and righteousness are.

> There is a way which seems right to a man, but its end is the way of death. (Proverbs 14:12 ISR)

> Everyone doing sin also does lawlessness, and sin is lawlessness. (1 John 3:4 ISR)

Sin against His Law/Torah leads to eternal death, which is the opposite of eternal life. Eternal death is complete and total separation *forever* from our Creator and from all the comfort, joy, and blessings He has planned for us. But we get to choose.

Contemplate what the exact opposite of being with Him will be. It's not a pretty picture. The opposite of eternal comfort is eternal pain and torment. The opposite of eternal joy is eternal sorrow. The opposite of eternal blessings is never-ending curses. Isn't this why our Creator went to such great lengths to give His only begotten Son for us? Weren't we bought with a price? Yet He gives us the choice in this short life of whether we accept His most costly gift and then walk in His ways, or not.

This life that we've been given is not all there is—it's only the beginning of a forever destiny. It will end with us being with our Maker, His Son, and their blessings *or* our life ends in a forever destiny of spending eternity with our enemy and the never-ending torment and torture that we will have chosen *and* *deserved* for walking away from our Heavenly Father

Our Creator is true to the Words He has spoken concerning not only His promises, for good, but also His promises for judgment and wrath that He *will* pour out on His enemies. True, He is love, but that's not all….

> Who can comprehend the power of your anger? Your

wrath is as awesome as the fear you deserve. (Psalm
90:11 NLT)

For by fire and by His sword יהוה shall judge all
flesh, and the slain of יהוה shall be many. (Isaiah
66:16 ISR)

And the next verse, I know I quoted earlier in this book, but
it is very important to remember exactly how one becomes an
enemy of our Creator.

Adulterers and adulteresses! Do you not know that
friendship with the world is enmity with Elohim?
Whoever therefore intends to be a friend of the world
makes himself an enemy of Elohim. (James 4:4 ISR)

Do not love the world nor that which is in the world.
If anyone loves the world, the love of the Father is not
in him. Because all that is in the world—the lust of
the flesh, the lust of the eyes, and the pride of life—is
not of the Father but is of the world. And the world
passes away, and the lust of it, but the one doing the
desire of Elohim remains forever. Little children, it is
the last hour. (1 John 2:15-18a ISR)

Loving our own ways more than His commands is exactly
where our enemy wants us as being friends of this world. And
our religious leaders and church denominations, for the most
part, have played right into Satan's hands when they teach the
Law has been abolished though it is the very definition of sin and
righteousness. If, then, the Law is viewed as obsolete, we have
no guideline for what is right and what is wrong, what is good or
what is evil, making it all too easy to feel we have nothing to repent of. So why should we change the way we have been living?

To recap, this deceived thinking believes the Law was for

another people in another time and does not apply to us now, so we can:

- worship when and how we want (Exodus 20:8-11)
- eat all the pork as well as other creatures that He did not design as food (Leviticus 11)
- dress however we desire (Deuteronomy 22:5)
- kill my offspring when I believe I have the right to my own body and the life of my unborn "fetus" (Leviticus 18:21)
- have sexual relations with whomever and whatever (Leviticus 18:1-30 and Deuteronomy 27:20-26)
- ignore the needs of the fatherless, the widow, and the stranger (Exodus 22:22 and Deuteronomy 27:19), dishonor my parents (Leviticus 19:3, Exodus 20:12, and Deuteronomy 27:16)

...and so on and on, all without consequence. Do you see what horrible reasoning this is? We have proudly and defiantly directed our own steps, becoming an enemy of our Creator while befriending the world as we embrace the things it says are okay! (Jeremiah 10:23)

This lawlessness in cooperating with the world and its ruler is explained even further in the parable of the sower in Matthew 13. Please read Matthew 13 from verse 1-50 in your copy of Scripture, and you will see what I'm talking about. Here I'll quote a few key verses concerning the "world." There is a connection between cooperating with the world and its ruler (our enemy) and doing lawlessness.

> And He answering, said to them, 'He who is sowing the good seed is the Son of Adam, and the field is the world. And the good seed, these are the sons of the reign, but the darnel are the sons of the wicked one,

and the enemy who sowed them is the devil. And the harvest is the end of the age, and the reapers are the messengers. As the darnel, then, is gathered and burned in the fire, so it shall be at the end of this age. The Son of Adam shall send out messengers, and they shall gather out of His reign all the stumbling-blocks, and those doing lawlessness, and shall throw them into the furnace of fire—there shall be wailing and gnashing of teeth. (Matthew 13:37-42 ISR)

…because everyone having been born of Elohim overcomes the world. And this is the overcoming that has overcome the world: our belief. (1 John 5:4 ISR)

Remember, it all starts with belief in the Son of our Creator, but it does not stop there—belief has action:

We know that everyone having been born of Elohim does not sin, but the one having been born of Elohim guards himself, and the wicked one does not touch him. (1 John 5:18 ISR)

If we believe in the abolishment of the Law, which shows us what sin is, we will easily become lovers of self, lovers of money, boastful, arrogant, abusive, disobedient to parents, un-grateful, wrongdoers, unloving, unforgiving, slanderers, without self-control, fierce, haters of good, betrayers, reckless, puffed up, and lovers of pleasure rather than lovers of our Heavenly Father. This is all because without the Law, we follow our own hearts and what is good in our own eyes instead. (See 2 Timothy 3:1-17 and 4:1-5)

We are commanded to come out of the world (out of pagan idolatrous Babylon) and the things that it loves as it does not pro-mote self-denial but rather it promotes self-pride, self-pleasure, self-expression, being true to yourself, trusting yourself, follow-ing your own heart, greed, lust of the flesh, and self-gratification.

We love our own ways more than we love our Maker's ways and place pleasing ourselves above pleasing Him as well as trusting and relying on ourselves more than we trust and rely on Him.

The verses below from the prophet Isaiah are just one example of how abominable it is for man to choose his own ways above his Maker's:

> *But* whoever slays the bull strikes a man, whoever slaughters the lamb breaks a dog's neck; whoever brings a grain offering—pig's blood; whoever burns incense blesses an idol. Indeed, they have chosen their own ways, and their being delights in their abominations. I shall also choose their punishments, and bring their fears on them. Because I called, but no one answered. I spoke and they did not hear, and they did evil before My eyes, and chose what was displeasing to Me. (Isaiah 66:3-4 ISR)

It is no different today than when our Creator first stated these words through Isaiah. Has He changed? And has mankind really improved in knowing and following Him?

It is not enough to be right in our own eyes; we have to be *right in His eyes according to His Word, His Law*. We must take Him and His commands seriously and know that in any area, whether we think it is big or small, if our heart leads us away, telling us that He is okay with even a little of our going astray or of excusing our behaviors and choices, then we have become wicked.

If you choose to walk in newness of life, of being led by your Creator and Heavenly Father through His Set-apart Spirit and not by men, you will be equipped to stand in His truth even in the face of trials and the testing of your faith.

> But my righteous one will live by faith; and if he shrinks back, my soul has no pleasure in him. But we are not among those who shrink back to destruction,

but of those who have faith for the safekeeping of the soul. (Hebrews 10:38-39 NASB)

As adamantly as I write all these things, I want you to know I still have areas in my life that my Maker is correcting as His Set-apart Spirit is prompting and teaching me every day how to love Him with all my heart. I know I have not arrived at all He has for me to learn. My goal is still (and I pray always will be) to strive for that completeness (Matthew 5:48), searching His Word for life's answers, letting Him connect the dots.

> Having, then, these promises, beloved, let us cleanse ourselves from all defilement of the flesh and spirit, perfecting set-apartness in the fear of Elohim. (2 Corinthians 7:1 ISR)

> Not that I have already received, or already been perfected, but I press on, to lay hold of that for which Messiah יהושע has also laid hold of me. (Philippians 3:12 ISR)

And remember, in the very beginning of this book I said, "This is personal." Here is another insight into the way I've always felt but rarely talk about. I have always had a very strong will, even from childhood. My mother said I was difficult to raise and this resulted in my being grounded and punished well into my teenage years. Ann, my best friend from childhood who continues to be my lifelong friend, can attest to this fact. So, when I think of or read the words "to stand," "to endure," "to overcome," they always strike a note in my spirit of defiance, a deviance against this world, an attitude to be an overcomer, to step to the beat of a different drummer, to not follow the crowd or what is popular. Praise the Father that my defiance and desire to deviate, to stand and to be a rebel, has been molded by Him in the right direction, which is towards Him and not away from Him!

Now, after living through and learning from several life lessons and prayerfully maturing in understanding my Father's Word, I am strongly opposed and very much against the ways of this world. I have turned my defiant spirit into a refusal to be desensitized, led, or controlled by the enemy of my soul and the deceit he tries to inflict in and through this world's agendas. I continue to watch out for what many today call "good." For example, the concepts of *unity* and *tolerance* sound all well and "good," especially in mass media and even sadly in many churches, but it is not the truth, because His Word speaks against the things that the world and media are calling us to tolerate. Isn't His Word like a sword that divides and sets apart from the world those who are being set apart by our Heavenly Father? When we step out of His design for living and loving, by believing the many lies we have inherited and call them "good," saying "I'm okay," and telling ourselves, "He is okay with my choices; this is how I feel," we are treading on dangerous ground. And feelings often cannot be trusted.

We need to especially think about what we believe—questioning what we have been taught, humbly running it through the timeless test of His Word with the leading of His Spirit, and finally comparing it with what the world is believing, teaching, and doing. All the while, know that our Heavenly Father's way to walk as His Son walked will never be popular.

Lies are increasingly being presented as truth. Remember that this practice began in the Garden. If you really want the truth, if it matters to you whether you have been lied to or not, then the only way to get out of this deceit is to humbly know Yahushua and the Word that He bears.

Keep in mind the truth that *all* of the written Word fits together from Genesis to Revelation, but it will not be evident to the casual believer or reader. From the books of the Law and the Prophets, writings like Psalms and Proverbs, to the writings of the apostles, *all* of the authors were chosen by our Creator to record His Words as well as to record, explain, and spread His Good News. And their writings and teachings do not contradict the everlasting existence and establishment of Yahuweh's plan for how His creation is to live and to love Him and each other, which is His Torah/His Law/His commandments. Satan wants to pick apart the Scripture so that he can twist its meaning and cause us to ignore the commands that are everlasting and that determine our allegiance and our forever destiny. All the books of Scripture tell of Yahuweh's unchanging righteousness. The more you read His words, the more truth you will know and the less lies you will believe so that you are able to stand, especially in the day of evil.

> Put on the complete armour of Elohim, for you to have power to stand against the schemes of the devil. Because we do not wrestle against flesh and blood, but against principalities, against authorities, against the world-rulers of the darkness of this age, against spiritual *matters* of wickedness in the heavenlies. Because of this, take up the complete armour of Elohim, so that you have power to withstand in the wicked day, and having done all, to stand. (Ephesians 6:11-13 ISR)

And now for the armor:

> Stand then, having girded your waist with truth, and having put on the breastplate of righteousness, and having fitted your feet with the preparation of the Good News of peace; above all, having taken up the shield of belief with which you shall have power to quench all the burning arrows of the wicked one. Take also the helmet of deliverance, and the sword of the Spirit, which is the Word of Elohim. (Ephesians 6:14-17 ISR)

I pray you are challenged to take a stand, to be an overcomer, to dig even deeper into your Heavenly Father's Word with more of an intensity and a searching after *Who* He is and what pleases Him than you have ever done in your life—because the truth matters!

And know that you will likely experience some trials and even loss as we have. But the trials make you stronger if you do not give up. There is nothing you can't overcome as He promises in His Word. I truly believe there is a calling going on, right now, that is being orchestrated by the Set-apart Spirit of Yahuweh. Believers are waking up to the Torah and Yahuweh's truths all over the United States, as well as all over the world, in cities and in small towns. While at the same time, many Jews are recognizing and turning to Yahushua for forgiveness and salvation. Truly, this is happening in a big way that can't be denied.

Many Christians, who are returning to Yahuweh's commands, call themselves "Messianic." Others call themselves "Torah Keepers," "Set-Apart Believers," "Sabbath Keepers," while others take on the identity of being called "Israel" (the name given to Jacob as he overcame). And we were asked, early on, as we began to keep the Sabbath and remove the pagan worship from our lives: "What do you call yourself?" I didn't know what to say. I had always identified myself as a "Christian" and was very proud of that. But eventually, as I began to see that most Christians do not believe in guarding Yahuweh's Sabbaths, and don't believe in obedience to His commanded Law/Torah, which really is antinomianism as discussed in detail earlier in this book, I knew I didn't want that label anymore. So now, I think of myself, simply, as a follower of Yahushua, truly learning to walk as He walked in His Father's way. And because of Him, I am grafted into the citizenship of Israel (Ephesians 2:10-19).

And if you are of Messiah, then you are seed of

Abraham, and heirs according to promise. (Galatians 3:29 ISR)

Some people are calling this mobilization of the Set-apart Spirit, "The Hebrew Roots Movement." And the waking up of many Jews to Yahushua is being called "The Messianic Jewish Movement." All I know is, it appears that the people who are waking up to the Torah (in particular to the seventh-day Sabbath and the commanded feasts of Leviticus 23), do not seem to be joining some movement to be part of a new religious experience or group. Instead, what I am observing is a much deeper work of the Set-apart Spirit. It's a calling by Yahuweh that I believe may also involve the spirit of Elijah, as he separated the true worshippers from the false, setting them apart. Think about it, to truly worship our Creator in both spirit and in truth, we wouldn't be okay with man changing His commandments! We would worship Him on His set-apart Sabbath day (the seventh day of the week that He blessed from the beginning in Genesis 2:3). We would also remove all the pagan traditions and symbols from our lives that we have inherited. We are being called out of Babylon (the ways of this world) to be set-apart in the way of our Heavenly Father and His Son.

Nations (Gentiles) have been coming into the citizenship of a spiritual Israel (Yahweh's chosen people) ever since the Messiah. And I do believe we are seeing a pouring out of the Set-apart Spirit today, because the days are getting darker and the time is getting shorter, before Yahushua's return. Even now, mainstream religious leaders do not deny that we are seeing the following downturn in our cultures:

> But know this, that in the last days, hard times shall come. For men shall be lovers of self, lovers of silver, boasters, proud, blasphemers, disobedient to parents, thankless, wrongdoers, unloving, unforgiving, slanderers, without self-control, fierce, haters of

good, betrayers, reckless, puffed up, lovers of
pleasure rather than lovers of Elohim, having a form
of reverences but denying its power. And turn away
from these! For among them are those who creep into
households and captivate silly women loaded down
with sins, led away by various lusts, always learning
and never able to come to the knowledge of the truth.
(2 Timothy 3:1-7 ISR)

And does the following prophecy not sound just like our
society today where people do not want to hear the truth of His
commands but only want to hear what tickles the ears, what is
smooth to listen to?

And go, write it before them on a tablet, and inscribe
it on a scroll, that it is for a latter day, a witness
forever: that this is a rebellious people, lying children,
children who refuse to hear the Torah of יהוה, who
say to the seers, 'Do not see,' and to the prophets, 'Do
not prophesy to us what is right. Speak to us what is
smooth, prophesy deceits. Turn aside from the way,
swerve from the path, cause the Set-apart One of
Yisra'el to cease from before us.' Therefore thus said
the Set-apart One of Yisra'el, 'Because you despise
this word, and trust in oppression and perverseness,
and rely on them, therefore this crookedness is to
you like a breach ready to fall, a bulge in a high wall,
whose breaking comes suddenly, swiftly,' and He
shall break it like the breaking of the potter's vessel,
which is broken in pieces, without sparing, so that
there is not found among its fragments a sherd to
take fire from the hearth, or to take water from the
cistern. For thus said the Master יהוה, the Set-apart
One of Yisra'el, 'In returning and rest you are saved,

in stillness and trust is your strength.' But you would not… (Isaiah 30:8-15 ISR)

I have been aware of the growing darkness for a long time. It is evident everywhere, even in the popular, seemingly innocent sitcoms that program us to laugh at the modern, worldly trends of today. I refuse to be desensitized into accepting these things since I have learned my Heavenly Father is seriously against them. I want His eyes, His heart, and to love what He loves and to hate what He hates.

After reading this book, if you choose to put your hand to the plow, to take a stand for His kingdom and its righteousness, to not look back in working out your salvation with fear and trembling, know as I have mentioned that you will have some persecutions (maybe even a lot of persecution), as He sets you apart from the ways of this world and its ruler. Sadly, many will choose to stay in the ways of this world and its temporary pleasures, but some will not. And to those who overcome, it's going to be worth it all, as I can hear Him saying to you on that final day, "Well done, good and faithful servant! Enter into the rest I have prepared for you. Your work is done."

Our prayer, and the main reason for this book, is to encourage you in your walk, as you discover more and more of His truths, in order to stand and overcome in this day in which you have been called to live. We also pray the experiences we have been through strengthen especially those who have just begun their journey on this narrow road. May you be inspired to walk as our Messiah walked in Spirit and in truth in the Way we were always meant to walk.

And you shall be set-apart to Me, for I יהוה am set-apart, and have separated you from the peoples to be Mine. (Leviticus 20:26 ISR)

This is what I long for, and it is the reason that I continue to search for the Truth that dispels the lies we have inherited…

RESOURCES & REFERENCES LIST

WEBSITES

https://www.biblehub.com/

https://biblesabbath.org/

https://torahfamily.org/

https://www.119ministries.com/

https://therefinersfire.org/

https://omniglot.com/

https://romeschallenge.com/

https://www.britannica.com/topic/Saturnalia-Roman-festival

https://www.newworldencyclopedia.org/p/index.php?title=Christmas&oldid=1032977

https://hymnary.org/hymn/TTvirt/168

https://www.merriam-webster.com/dictionary/antinomianism

https://youtu.be/R8T87C0cd6Q

https://youtu.be/-nkJg8tPSOg

https://youtu.be/P-QYn7S7qow

https://www.logosapostolic.org/bible_study/RP208-2ThreeDaysNights.htm

http://wordofyahuweh.weebly.com/easter-sunrise-service.html

https://www.gotquestions.org/temple-veil-torn.html

http://amazinghealth.com/AH-health-unclean-animals-pig-fish-mammals

https://www.offthegridnews.com/off-grid-foods/gods-dietary-laws-why-pigs-crabs-and-lobstersare-bad-for-you/

http://www.uncleanfoodsdietarylaws.com/unclean_foods_dietary_laws.html

https://www.bing.com/translator?ref=TThis&&text=a%20sign%20is%20a%20mark&from=&to=he

http://earthsky.org/astronomy-essentials/everything-you-need-to-know-vernal-or-spring-equinox.

BOOKS

Koster, Dr. C. J. *Come Out of Her, My People*. Institute for Scripture Research, Ltd. 1st edition (January 1, 2004).

The New Strong's Exhaustive Concordance of the Bible, by James Strong, LL.D., S.T.D. Thomas Nelson Publishers (1990)

ARTICLES AND OTHER REFERENCE MATERIALS

Holloway, April. "Pagan Gods and the naming of the days." https://www.ancient-origins.net/myths-legends/pagan-gods-and-naming-days-001037

"The True Set Apart Name of the Creator is יהוה or YHWH (YaHuWaH)." Warriors Of The Ruwach. **https://warriorsoftheruwach.com/en/yahuwah**

"Why Is God's Name Missing From Many Bibles?" **https://researchsupportsthetruth.wordpress.com/2013/07/08/why-is-gods-name-missing-from-many-bibles/**

"The Divisions of the Scriptures." **https://biblehub.com/library/gerberding/the_way_of_salvation_in_the_lutheran_church/chapter_v_the_divisions_of.htm**

John Wesley and the Conference of 1744 (imarc.cc) – **https://www.imarc.cc/reghist/reghist3.html**

"Did Abraham Keep the Same Commandments God Gave to Moses?" United Church of God (ucg.org) **https://www.ucg.org/bible-study-tools/booklets/the-new-covenant-does-it-abolish-gods-law/did-abraham-keep-the-same-commandments-god-gave-to-moses**

https://www.biblestudytools.com/encyclopedias/isbe/partition-the-middle-wall-of.html

Strong's Concordance, Hebrew: 3068. (Yhvh) the proper name of the God of Israel – **https://biblehub.com/hebrew/3068.htm**

Strong's Concordance, Greek: 1520. εἷς (*heis*) one – **https://biblehub.com/greek/1520.htm**

Strong's Concordance, Greek: 4520. σαββατισμός, οῦ, ὁ (*sabbatismos*) a sabbath rest – **https://biblehub.com/greek/4520.htm**

Thayer's Greek Lexicon: 4137. πληρόω (*pléroó*) to make full, to complete – **https://biblehub.com/thayers/4137.htm**

Thayer's Greek Lexicon: 2647. καταλύω (*kataluó*) to deprive of force, annul, abrogate, discard – **https://biblehub.com/thayers/2647.htm**

Thayer's Greek Lexicon: 5565. χωρίς (*chóris*) separately, apart – **https://biblehub.com/greek/5565.htm**

Strong's Exhaustive Concordance: 226. אוֹת (*oth*) mark, miracle, ensign – **https://biblehub.com/hebrew/226.htm**

While the books and websites I've used in the writing of this book were helpful and I have directly referred to most of them, I want to make it clear that we do not follow everything contained within them. It is imperative to test everything against our Maker's written Word, that I often refer to as His *Scriptures,* coupled with a humble and fearful leading of His Set-apart Spirit.

BIBLE BOOKS AND OTHER TRANSLATION BOOKS QUOTED

Institute for Scripture Research (ISR)

King James Version (KJV)

New King James Version (NKJV)

New International Version (NIV)

Holman Christian Standard Bible

English Standard Version (ESV)

New American Standard Bible (NASB)

Aramaic Bible in Plain English

Berean Study Bible

New Living Translation (NLT)

Contemporary English Version (CEV)

Jubilee Bible 2000

King James 2000 Bible

Berean Literal Bible

Christian Standard Bible

Good News Translation

International Standard Version

American King James Version

Webster's Bible Translation

Young's Literal Translation

ACKNOWLEDGEMENTS

To Conner and Celesta Stevens who told me that the greatest thing they could teach me was to learn to search the Scriptures for myself. I am grateful that you took the time and patience to do this. Now I pray that I am able to pass this practice on to many others in the writing of this book.

To Peggy and Michael, my dear friends who came into my life only within the last few years. Thank you for always being that willing and humble sounding board as you helped me with the writing of several of my chapters. I have so enjoyed searching and researching the Scriptures for the truth with you.

ABOUT THE AUTHOR

Lenora Hoag has been married to her husband Kevin for over 40 years. They have three daughters and four grandchildren and have been caregivers for each other's parents while working on their small Texas farm.

Her deeply rooted passion for ministry, missions, and teaching has always included family, friends, and her community, which led to a degree in Social Work and working for over twelve years with adults who had developmental disabilities and then serving the senior community through home health and hospice vocations. Although officially retired, Lenora continues to work for her family while enjoying her love of cooking, camping, and trying new adventures, especially with her grandchildren.

Hoag's number one passion is reading and researching the Scriptures and then sharing, especially through her writing, their treasure of wisdom, direction, love, and warning that we all need in order to love our Maker with all our hearts and to love each other as He has designed.

CPSIA information can be obtained
at www.ICGtesting.com
Printed in the USA
BVHW031931121221
623864BV00005B/114